Grant Writing Mastery

A Complete Guide to Getting Funding and Writing Winning Proposals for Nonprofits, Community Programs, and Creative Projects

Hoong Yee Lee

© Copyright 2024 - All rights reserved.

The content contained within this book may not be reproduced, duplicated or transmitted without direct written permission from the author or the publisher.

Under no circumstances will any blame or legal responsibility be held against the publisher, or author, for any damages, reparation, or monetary loss due to the information contained within this book, either directly or indirectly.

Legal Notice:

This book is copyright protected. It is only for personal use. You cannot amend, distribute, sell, use, quote or paraphrase any part, or the content within this book, without the consent of the author or publisher.

Disclaimer Notice:

Please note the information contained within this document is for educational and entertainment purposes only. All effort has been executed to present accurate, up to date, reliable, complete information. No warranties of any kind are declared or implied. Readers acknowledge that the author is not engaged in the rendering of legal, financial, medical or professional advice. The content within this book has been derived from various sources. Please consult a licensed professional before attempting any techniques outlined in this book.

By reading this document, the reader agrees that under no circumstances is the author responsible for any losses, direct or indirect, that are incurred as a result of the use of the information contained within this document, including, but not limited to, errors, omissions, or inaccuracies.

Table of Contents

INTRODUCTION 3
    WHAT'S INSIDE: A SNEAK PEEK INTO MASTERING GRANT WRITING 5
    HOW TO USE THIS BOOK: YOUR ROADMAP TO GRANT WRITING SUCCESS 7

CHAPTER 1: THE WONDERFUL WORLD OF GRANTS 9
    GRANTS 101: WHAT THEY ARE AND WHY YOU WANT ONE 9
        Basic Definitions and Concepts 9
        The Benefits of Grant Funding 11
    THE GRANT UNIVERSE: TYPES OF GRANTS AND WHICH ONES MAKES A DIFFERENCE IN THE WORLD 13
        Overview of Different Types of Grants 13
        Matching Your Needs to the Right Type of Grant 15
    DEBUNKING COMMON GRANT WRITING MYTHS 17
    ACTION ITEMS 19

CHAPTER 2: KNOW THYSELF (AND THY PROJECT) 21
    SPECIFYING YOUR MISSION: WHAT DO YOU WANT TO ACCOMPLISH? 21
        Exercises for Defining Your Mission and Vision 21
        Clarifying Your Project Goals and Objectives 22
    PROJECT PLANNING: TURNING IDEAS INTO FUNDABLE PROJECTS 24
        Steps for Developing a Solid Project Plan 24
        Tools for Project Management and Planning 26
    ACTION ITEMS 27

CHAPTER 3: FINDING YOUR PERFECT MATCH 29
    GRANT HUNTING: FINDING AND CHOOSING THE RIGHT GRANTS 29
        Research Available Grant Opportunities 29
        Leverage Networks and Local Resources 29
        Evaluate Grant Opportunities 30
    NETWORKING LIKE A PRO: DEVELOPING SOLID RELATIONSHIPS WITH FUNDERS 31
        Tips for Effective Networking and Relationship-Building 31
        How to Communicate With Funders 33
    TOOLS OF THE TRADE: DIGITAL RESOURCES AND GRANT DATABASES 33
        Overview of Useful Tools and Databases 34
        How to Leverage Technology for Grant Writing Success 35
        Examples of Success 36
    ACTION ITEMS 37

CHAPTER 4: RESEARCH AND PREPARATION 39
    UNDERSTANDING GRANT GUIDELINES: READING BETWEEN THE LINES 39

- Decoding and Interpreting Grant Guidelines 39
- Tips for Ensuring Compliance With Funder Requirements 41
- Real-World Success: Before-and-After Examples 42
- THE ART OF RESEARCH: KNOW YOUR FUNDER AND THEIR PRIORITIES 43
  - Techniques for Researching Funders 43
  - Case Studies of Successful Research Strategies 44
- GATHERING YOUR TEAM: WHO YOU NEED AND WHY 45
  - Identifying Key Team Members for Grant Writing 45
  - Roles and Responsibilities in the Grant Writing Process 47
- ACTION ITEMS 47

CHAPTER 5: WRITING WITH STYLE (AND SUBSTANCE) **49**

- PROPOSAL WRITING BASICS: STRUCTURE AND FLOW 49
  - Standard Components of a Grant Proposal 49
  - Organizing Your Proposal for Maximum Impact 52
- COMPOSING A PERSUASIVE NARRATIVE: STORYTELLING IN GRANT WRITING 53
  - Techniques for Engaging Storytelling 54
  - Examples of Compelling Narratives 55
- SIMPLIFYING YOUR LANGUAGE: CLEAR AND CONCISE COMMUNICATION 56
  - Suggestions for Straightforward and Succinct Writing 56
  - Familiar Jargon Pitfalls and How to Avoid Them 57
  - Tips on Presenting Yourself or Your Organization Compellingly 58
- ACTION ITEMS 59

CHAPTER 6: THE CORE COMPONENTS **61**

- STATEMENT OF NEED: DEFINING THE NEED 61
- PURPOSES AND GOALS: WHAT YOU STRIVE TO ACCOMPLISH 62
  - Aligning Your Project With Funder Priorities 62
- METHODS AND ACTIVITIES: HOW YOU'LL DO IT 64
- EVALUATION PLANS: MEASURING SUCCESS 64
- BUDGETS: SHOW ME THE MONEY! 66
- ACTION ITEMS 67

CHAPTER 7: POLISHING YOUR PROPOSAL **69**

- POLISH YOUR PROPOSAL WITH EFFECTIVE EDITING TIPS 69
  - Practical Techniques for Editing and Proofreading 69
  - Common Mistakes to Watch Out For 70
- VISUAL AIDS: USING CHARTS, GRAPHS, AND IMAGES 72
  - How to Incorporate Visual Aids Effectively 72
  - Examples of Impactful Visuals 73
- GETTING FEEDBACK: THE MORE EYES, THE BETTER 74
  - Strategies for Soliciting and Incorporating Feedback 75
  - The Power of Many Eyes 75
- ACTION ITEMS 76

CHAPTER 8: SUBMISSION SUCCESS 77
DIGITAL SUBMISSIONS: NAVIGATING ONLINE PORTALS 77
Tips for Successful Digital Submissions 77
Common Issues and How to Avoid Them 78
PAPER SUBMISSIONS: WHEN OLD SCHOOL STILL RULES 79
Best Practices for Paper Submissions 79
Ensuring Your Submission Stands Out 80
FOLLOW-UP ETIQUETTE: STAYING ON THE FUNDER'S RADAR 81
Building Ongoing Relationships With Funders 81
ACTION ITEMS 82

CHAPTER 9: THE WAITING GAME 83
WHAT TO DO WHILE YOU WAIT: TAKING CONTROL OF THE WAITING PERIOD 83
Productive Activities During the Waiting Period 83
Preparing for Possible Outcomes 84
SITE VISITS: SHOWCASING YOUR ORGANIZATION'S IMPORTANCE 85
Tips for Hosting Site Visits 85
Making a Positive Impression on Funders 87
HANDLING REJECTIONS: BOUNCING BACK STRONGER 88
Dealing With Rejection Positively 88
Learning From Feedback and Improving Future Proposals 89
ACTION ITEMS 90

CHAPTER 10: WHEN YOU WIN 93
CELEBRATING SUCCESS: SHARING THE GOOD NEWS 93
Announcing Your Grant Win 93
Engaging Stakeholders and Supporters 94
MANAGING GRANT FUNDS: BEST PRACTICES 95
Effective Grant Fund Management 95
Ensuring Compliance and Accountability 96
REPORTING AND COMPLIANCE: KEEPING FUNDERS HAPPY 96
Developing Comprehensive Reports 97
Maintaining Good Relationships With Funders 97
ACTION ITEMS 98

CHAPTER 11: BEYOND THE GRANT 101
SUSTAINABILITY: PLANNING FOR LIFE AFTER THE GRANT 101
Strategies for Sustaining Your Project Post-Grant 101
Diversifying Funding Sources 102
BUILDING LONG-TERM RELATIONSHIPS WITH FUNDERS 103
Tips for Long-Term Engagement With Funders 104
Turning Funders Into Long-Term Partners 104
CONTINUOUS IMPROVEMENT: LEARNING FROM EACH EXPERIENCE 105

  Reflecting On and Learning From Each Grant Cycle *105*
  Using Feedback to Improve Future Proposals *106*
 ACTION ITEMS 107

CONCLUSION **109**

 STAYING IN TOUCH: JOINING THE GRANT WRITING COMMUNITY 109
 ADDITIONAL RESOURCES TO KEEP YOU GROWING 111
  Blogs *111*
  Workshops *111*
 FINAL THOUGHTS 112

THANK YOU! **113**

APPENDIX **115**

 A. SAMPLE OF GRANT FINAL REPORT TEMPLATE 115
 B. PROJECT PLANNING EXAMPLES 116
  Example of a SWOT Analysis *116*
  Example of Story Mapping *119*
  Example of a Detailed Project Description *120*
  Example of a Poorly Written Budget *125*
  Example of a Well-Written Budget *126*
  Example of a Pie Chart *128*
  Example of a Timeline *128*
  Example of an Evaluation Plan *130*
 C. GRANT APPLICATION CHECKLIST TEMPLATE 133
  Grant Application Checklist *133*
 D. EXAMPLE OF AN EVALUATION PLAN 135
  Process Evaluation *135*
  Results Evaluation *136*
 E. LETTER OF SUPPORT SAMPLE 141

REFERENCES **142**

For Seth

Introduction

Picture this scenario: Suppose you're setting off on a treasure hunt, and instead of a pirate's map, you hold a grant proposal in your hands. You're in a dimly lit room, hunched over your laptop, the cursor blinking at you like a skeptical judge. You sip your cold coffee, take a deep breath, and dive in, weaving your project's story with the finesse of a novelist and the precision of a surgeon. You hit "submit" and wait, feeling like Indiana Jones having just dodged a rolling boulder. Weeks later, you get the email—you've secured the funding! It's the modern-day equivalent of discovering a chest of gold doubloons. Welcome to the thrilling world of grant writing, where every proposal is a new adventure, and the reward is your dreams becoming reality.

Many grant seekers have brilliant ideas but need more resources. This is where grant writing steps in. It's like embarking on a quest; the ultimate reward is the funding and support you need to bring your vision to life. The process might seem daunting at first, but trust me, it's worth every effort.

Imagine you're a scientist with a groundbreaking research idea that could change how we understand climate change. You need funding to buy equipment, hire assistants, and conduct experiments. A compelling grant proposal can secure the resources to turn your hypothesis into published findings.

Or maybe you're a passionate community member who dreams of starting a community garden to provide neighbors with a gathering space and fresh produce. A grant can cover the costs of land, seeds, tools, and educational workshops, transforming an empty lot into a vibrant green oasis.

You may be involved with an existing nonprofit program that supports at-risk youth. You see the potential to expand your services to reach more kids, but the budget is tight. A grant can provide the funds needed for additional staff, new activities, and better resources to make a more significant impact.

Consider starting a summer concert series to bring music and joy to your town. A grant can help you book bands, rent sound equipment, and promote the events, creating unforgettable experiences for your community.

Finally, imagine running a local food bank struggling to meet increasing demand. With a grant, you can expand your storage capacity, buy more food, and serve more families, ensuring no one in your area goes hungry.

Whether seeking funding for innovative research, starting a community garden, supporting an existing program, launching a summer concert series, expanding a local food bank, or any other project, grant writing opens doors to possibilities that can transform dreams into reality.

From my journey, I can tell you that the thrill of receiving that "Congratulations, you've been funded!" email is unmatched. It combines relief, joy, and a massive sense of accomplishment. Seeing your vision recognized and financially backed by others is incredibly empowering. It's not just about the money—it's the validation that your ideas matter, that they are seen and respected by a wider community of changemakers.

Every application you submit is a step toward enhancing your skills and boosting your likelihood of success. Each rejection teaches you something new, and each success builds your confidence. Learning and growing bring immense joy throughout this journey. With every grant proposal, you seek funding and refine your ability to tell your story compellingly and persuasively. Remember, even rejections are valuable insights that can enhance your future applications.

The grant writing process is challenging but incredibly rewarding. It's a testament to your commitment and acknowledgment of your hard work. So, let's dive in, embrace the journey, and remember that each step brings us closer to turning our dreams into reality. This is a journey that encourages and fuels determination.

Grant Writing Mastery: A Complete Guide to Getting Funding and Writing Winning Proposals for Nonprofits, Community Programs, and Creative Projects simplifies the grant writing process, offering valuable advice and insider secrets from an experienced grant reviewer. We'll debunk myths, highlight before-and-after examples, and point out common pitfalls to avoid. By understanding these real-world scenarios, you'll gain insights into what works and what doesn't, helping you refine your approach. This guide will give you the knowledge and tools to navigate the dynamic world of grants confidently and succeed.

What's Inside: A Sneak Peek Into Mastering Grant Writing

Jump into the essentials of grant writing with this insightful guide. Packed with valuable information, it debunks common myths and provides practical tips to help you secure funding for your projects. Let's look at what you'll learn and how it can transform your approach to grant writing.

You'll start with the fundamentals and explore the dynamic world of grants. Understanding what grants are and why you want one is crucial. Grants give you and your organization a significant financial boost. Still, it's important to remember that there's no such thing as free money. Every grant comes with specific requirements and expectations that you must meet.

Planning and researching are essential steps in developing a grant proposal. You must clearly define your goals, align them with the grantmaker's priorities, and demonstrate how your project will make a meaningful impact. Effective grant writing is about crafting a compelling narrative that convinces funders that their investment in your project is beneficial.

You'll also discover the various types of grants and learn how to align your needs with the appropriate ones. Understanding the landscape of grantmakers, from foundations to corporate philanthropies and government agencies to national and local nonprofits, is crucial.

This book will bust common grant writing myths, highlighting that you don't need to hire a professional grant writer, you're not too small to apply to a large foundation, and foundations are approachable and eager to hear from new applicants. By debunking these misconceptions, you'll gain the confidence to tackle grant writing yourself, understand that even small organizations can successfully secure large grants, and realize that building relationships with foundations is entirely possible.

Knowing yourself and your project is essential. This book helps you craft a compelling story for you or your organization and define your mission clearly. You'll learn to align your project goals with funder priorities and turn your ideas into fundable projects. You'll use project planning tools and techniques to ensure your proposals are well-structured and compelling.

Finding the right grant involves strategic searching and evaluating potential opportunities. Networking is not just important; it's critical, and this book provides tips on building relationships with funders and effectively communicating your mission. You'll also discover helpful digital resources and grant databases that can streamline your grant-hunting process. It's all about building connections and being part of a community of grantmakers and grant seekers.

Successful grant writing hinges on thorough research and preparation. Knowledge of grant guidelines and decoding funder requirements saves time and boosts your odds of success. The art of researching funders and gathering a capable team is also covered, ensuring you have the right people to support your grant writing efforts.

Writing with style and substance is another focus. This book teaches you the standard components of a grant proposal and how to organize it for maximum impact. Crafting a compelling narrative and avoiding jargon are emphasized, with examples and tips to keep your writing clear and engaging. You'll learn to articulate your project's problem, set SMART goals, detail your methods, and develop effective evaluation plans. Creating realistic and compelling budgets is also discussed, providing the financial clarity needed for your proposals.

Polishing your proposal is the final touch before submission. The book covers effective editing techniques, visual aids, and strategies for soliciting feedback. Whether you're submitting digitally or on paper, the book provides best practices to ensure your submission stands out.

We will also cover follow-up etiquette, ensuring you know how to maintain professional relationships with funders.

After you submit your proposal, you enter the waiting phase. The book offers productive activities to keep you busy and prepare for possible outcomes. It also discusses hosting site visits, handling rejections, and celebrating success. When you win a grant, managing the funds effectively and ensuring compliance is critical. This book provides best practices for grant fund management and reporting to assure funders they have invested wisely in you and your project.

Looking beyond the grant, sustainability planning, and building long-term relationships with funders are crucial for continued success. This guide will emphasize the importance of continuous improvement, urging you to learn from each experience to enhance your grant writing skills and create more vital proposals in the future. *Grant Writing Mastery: A Complete Guide to Getting Funding and Writing Winning Proposals for Nonprofits, Community Programs, and Creative Projects* thoroughly prepares you to master the challenges of grant writing and secure essential funding for your projects.

How to Use This Book: Your Roadmap to Grant Writing Success

To get the most out of this book, consider it your go-to guide for mastering grant writing. Start by familiarizing yourself with the layout. Each chapter builds on the previous one, so following the sequence is essential. Work through the exercises—they solidify your knowledge and enable you to apply it to real-world situations. Don't just read through them—actively engage and practice. Use the resources provided, from templates to checklists, to streamline your process. Keep them handy, as they are invaluable tools.

Approach the book with a mindset geared toward practical application. Take notes, mark important points, and revisit sections as needed. Treat it like a workshop where you learn by doing. The goal is to understand grant writing and become proficient at it. Stay committed to the exercises and use the resources consistently. This approach will boost your confidence and skills, enabling you to create compelling grant proposals efficiently. Make this book your constant companion on your grant writing journey, and you'll find yourself navigating the complexities efficiently and successfully.

Now that you have a solid grasp of navigating this book, it's time to dive into the nuts and bolts of grant writing. Let's start with the basics and build your foundation in grant writing, ensuring you're well-prepared to tackle your first proposal confidently.

Chapter 1:

The Wonderful World of Grants

Imagine you're on a treasure hunt. Instead of gold doubloons, you're after something even more valuable: funding for your big idea. You've got the map (your project plan), and the X marks the spot (the perfect grant). The catch? The treasure chest is locked, and the key is a well-crafted grant proposal. You've got to charm the guardians of the gold (the grant reviewers) with your wit, wisdom, and a compelling story. It's not just about finding the treasure—it's about proving you're worthy of it.

Now that you're intrigued by the treasure hunt, let's dive into the basics. The following section will teach you what grants are and why they're the key to unlocking the funding you need.

Grants 101: What They Are and Why You Want One

Grants can be game-changers for your projects, supplying a valuable financial boost. You'll discover what grants are, why they're worth pursuing, and how they can transform your ideas into reality. Get ready to learn about these funding opportunities and unlock your potential!

Basic Definitions and Concepts

A grant can fund an individual, nonprofit, or other qualifying entity to support specific projects or initiatives. Unlike loans, grants are highly attractive because you don't have to repay them. They support various activities, including scientific research, educational programs, community development, and artistic endeavors.

For example, the Peter H. & Dana Gunn Winslow Foundation (URL: hunnwinslowfoundation.org) focuses on providing grants to programs that support under-resourced children, particularly in education and health. They aim to empower these children by offering opportunities and resources that might otherwise be unavailable, helping to create a more equitable future for them. The US Chess Federation (URL: new.uschess.org) provides grants to enhance chess education for underprivileged youth, supplying financial support for equipment and school educational programs.

Grants come with detailed requirements for spending and reporting to ensure accountability and proper use of funds. For instance, the National Science Foundation (NSF; URL: nsf.gov) mandates grantees submit annual and final project reports, including financial reports detailing expenditures in line with the approved budget. Grantees must also demonstrate that they used the funds effectively to meet the grant's objectives by providing data on project outcomes and impact. These reports are typically due within 90 days after the grant's expiration, ensuring that the project stayed within the scope of the original proposal and complied with NSF guidelines.

Note: Please check Appendix A for the sample Grant Final Report. You can head to Smartsheet to download the template (URL: smartsheet.com/free-grant-proposal-templates).

Moreover, grant funding has a substantial impact. In 2021, U.S. federal grants alone accounted for $1.121 trillion, funding vital services like healthcare, education, and infrastructure (*What Types*, n.d.). Thus, navigating the grant landscape can unlock significant resources to drive your projects forward.

For individuals, grants can provide essential support for pursuing personal projects or research. For example, small business grants can help entrepreneurs launch and sustain their ventures, significantly impacting their success and growth potential. Grants for individuals can also include disaster relief funding for those affected by natural calamities, travel grants for academic or cultural exchanges, debt relief for financial stability, grants for creating new works in the arts, and funding for hiring consultants to provide expert guidance on specialized projects.

Small organizations benefit immensely from grant funding by gaining the financial stability needed to expand their services and outreach. These grants frequently cover operational expenses, enabling organizations to concentrate on carrying out their projects. For instance, local nonprofits might receive community grants to support staff positions in neighborhood revitalization projects and extend their programs into new neighborhoods.

Large organizations, while often having more resources, rely on significant grants to fund large-scale projects and research initiatives. These grants can help organizations achieve substantial milestones, like developing new technologies or implementing wide-reaching social programs. Foundations like the Ford and Robert Wood Johnson Foundation (URL: rwjf.org) provide generous operating grants to support these expansive efforts.

By understanding the impact of grants on different scales, you can better appreciate their importance and strategically navigate the grant landscape to identify the best funding source for your projects.

The Benefits of Grant Funding

Securing a grant can provide numerous benefits that significantly advance your projects and initiatives. Here's how:

Financial Support

Grants provide substantial financial support without requiring repayment. This lets you focus on your project rather than worrying about generating revenue to cover costs. Research funded by grants often results in groundbreaking discoveries that might not have been achievable otherwise. This funding can lead to significant medical advancements, such as the development of new vaccines and therapies. This financial support can make a crucial difference in fields requiring substantial investment, such as scientific research, educational programs, and community development initiatives.

Financial support from grants offers individuals numerous benefits beyond just funding their projects. For instance, grants can provide vital resources to artists, enabling them to create without the financial pressure of selling their work immediately. This freedom allows for more innovative and risk-taking endeavors, which can lead to significant contributions in the arts.

In the case of disaster relief, grants can provide immediate assistance to individuals affected by natural disasters, covering essential needs such as housing, food, and medical care. This timely support can help individuals rebuild their lives faster, reducing the long-term impact of such events.

For students and researchers, travel grants can open doors to opportunities for international collaboration, conference attendance, and access to specialized training. These experiences can significantly enhance their professional development and broaden their perspectives, leading to personal and career growth.

Moreover, grants for educational programs can directly benefit individuals by providing scholarships, stipends, or resources that enable them to pursue higher education or specialized training. This financial support can make education accessible to those who might otherwise be unable to afford it, ultimately leading to more significant opportunities and upward mobility.

Overall, grants empower individuals by providing the financial support needed to pursue passions, advance careers, and contribute meaningfully to their communities and fields of interest.

Credibility and Recognition

Receiving a grant enhances your credibility and reputation, signaling to potential funders, partners, and stakeholders that your project merits investment and makes securing additional funding and support more accessible. Organizations receiving grants from prestigious foundations experience increased visibility and credibility, leading to more funding opportunities. Moreover, being recognized by notable grant providers like the Bill & Melinda Gates Foundation or the Ford Foundation can significantly boost your project's profile.

Innovation and Impact

Grants often support innovative projects that substantially impact society, driving progress in various fields. For example, the American Express philanthropy program (URL: americanexpress.com/en-us/company/corporate-sustainability/community-impact/apply-grant/) provides substantial funding through multiple initiatives. One such program, the "Backing Historic Small Restaurants" grant, helps small, independent restaurants improve their physical spaces and cover critical operating costs, enhancing their community impact. This program, part of the larger "Backing Small" initiative, aims to preserve cultural heritage and support local economies by investing in community-focused businesses (*American Express*, 2023).

These benefits illustrate why pursuing grants is strategic for any individual or small organization grant seeker. You can achieve remarkable outcomes and make a difference by leveraging grants' financial support, credibility, and innovation potential.

The Grant Universe: Types of Grants and Which Ones Makes a Difference in the World

Navigating the grant universe may seem overwhelming, but finding the right grant for your needs is crucial. Understanding different types of grants, from government to private sources, enables you to make informed decisions. Explore these options to find the grant that best aligns with your goals.

Overview of Different Types of Grants

There are several types of grants, each serving different purposes and audiences. Understanding the distinctions between these grants can help you pinpoint the best opportunities for your needs. Let's discuss some common types:

Government Grants

Federal, state, or local governments typically provide these grants to support public services, economic development, and research. For example, the New York State Council on the Arts (NYSCA; URL: arts.ny.gov) funds nonprofit arts organizations across New York to improve cultural education, community development, and artistic innovation. These grants support various activities, including exhibitions, performances, and educational programs, contributing to the cultural enrichment of local communities.

Foundation Grants

Private and community foundations grant funds to support various charitable activities, and these foundations differ significantly in size and scope. Small local foundations often focus on projects specific to their communities. For instance, The Bronx Community Foundation (URL: thebronx.org) improves the lives of Bronx residents by supporting education, health, economic development, and social services initiatives.

The Rockefeller Foundation and other large entities fund global health and development initiatives. For instance, the Rockefeller Foundation (URL: rockefellerfoundation.org) committed over $1 billion to climate resilience and renewable energy projects to combat climate change and support sustainable development worldwide (*The Rockefeller Foundation*, 2023). Foundation grants are often more flexible than government grants, offering excellent opportunities to secure funding for innovative or niche projects.

Corporate Grants

Many corporations have philanthropic divisions providing grants for community development, education, and other causes. These grants benefit the community and enhance the company's Corporate Social Responsibility (CSR) image. For example, Walmart's Spark Good Local Grants (URL: walmart.com/nonprofits/) provides funds ranging from $250 to $5,000 to nonprofit initiatives that address local community needs, such as creating opportunities, advancing sustainability, and strengthening community ties. Eligible organizations can apply for these grants every quarter, ensuring regular access and availability (*Free Grants*, 2024). Securing corporate grants can also lead to valuable partnerships and further support beyond the initial funding.

Nonprofit Grants

Numerous nonprofit organizations offer grants aligning with their missions, often focusing on areas like the arts, environment, or social justice. For example, the Clif Family Foundation (URL: cliffamilyfoundation.org) grants small nonprofits for projects that promote community health, strengthen food systems, and protect the environment, focusing on operational support and specific initiatives with strong community involvement and viable plans for change (*Our Grants Program*, n.d.).

To identify the right grant type for your needs, understand the different funding sources and their specific focus areas. Government, foundation, corporate, and nonprofit grants present unique opportunities and challenges. Researching and targeting the proper grants will significantly increase your chances of finding the right fit for your project funding.

Matching Your Needs to the Right Type of Grant

To determine which grant is right for you, follow these crucial steps:

Step 1: Identify Your Needs

Begin by distinctly describing what you need funding for. Do you need financing for operational costs, a specific project, research, or something else? Knowing your exact needs helps you target suitable grants. For example, a small nonprofit organization like "Art for All," which provides free art classes to underserved youth, might seek funding to expand its program. By identifying their need for additional art supplies, instructor salaries, and venue costs, they can target grants designed explicitly for community enrichment and youth programs. They might apply for a grant from the National Endowment for the Arts or a local foundation like the Cleveland Foundation (URL: clevelandfoundation.org), which offers community grants focused on arts and culture initiatives.

Step 2: Research Potential Grants

Search for grants that match your needs and goals. Explore online databases such as Grants.gov (URL: grants.gov), Foundation Center (URL: fconline.foundationcenter.org), and corporate websites to find opportunities. Grants.gov offers a comprehensive list of federal grant opportunities and tools to check eligibility and search for specific grants.

Insider tip: Look at who else is doing what you want to do. Check their websites to see who funds them. For example, if you're seeking a grant to start a community garden, visit the websites of similar local projects to find their funding sources. For example, the Detroit Black Community Food Security Network (URL: dbcfsn.org) lists its funders on its website, including regional and national organizations such as the Kresge Foundation (URL: kresge.org) and the W.K. Kellogg Foundation (URL: wkkf.org). This method helps identify potential funders who are likely to support projects similar to yours.

Step 3: Understand the Requirements

Carefully review each grant's eligibility criteria, application process, and reporting requirements. Ensure you can meet these before applying. Many grants require specific fund usage and reporting guidelines, including maintaining detailed financial records and providing progress reports.

For example, most grants have particular eligibility criteria. The National Endowment for the Arts (URL: arts.gov) requires that applicants be nonprofit, tax-exempt 501(c)(3) organizations, state or local government units, or federally recognized tribal communities or tribes . Meanwhile, small business grants from the U.S. Small Business Administration (SBA; URL: sba.gov) may require applicants to meet specific size standards and demonstrate a need for financial assistance due to economic hardship .

Similarly, the eligibility criteria for the Awesome Foundation (URL: awesomefoundation.org/en/) grants focus on projects that promote awesomeness in the universe. Still, they specifically exclude funding for travel, land purchases, and businesses whose sole purpose is to generate revenue .

Understanding these specifics ensures you direct your efforts toward grants for which you are eligible, ultimately saving you precious time.

Debunking Common Grant Writing Myths

Many people hold onto myths and misconceptions about grant writing, which can mislead them and reduce their chances of obtaining crucial project funding. Let's dispel some familiar myths and expose the truths about successful grant writing.

Myth 1: Grants Are Easy Money

Many people think grants are easy money, but writing a grant proposal requires dedication, meticulous planning, thorough research, and a clear understanding of the funder's criteria. You must show that you and your organization are deserving of valuable investments. Grants are not a quick fix; they demand extensive preparation and diligent follow-through, emphasizing your commitment to your cause.

Myth 2: A Standard Proposal Works for All Grants

Creating and using one generic proposal for multiple grant applications might seem like a good idea. However, nothing could be further from the truth. Each grantmaker has specific priorities and requirements, and your proposal needs to address these unique elements. Tailoring each proposal to fit the particular funder's guidelines increases your chances of success. While you can reuse specific components like your organization's mission statement, you must tailor much of the content for each application.

Myth 3: Grant Writers Work on Commission

Contrary to popular belief, professional grant writers do not work on commission. Grantmakers view this practice as unethical because it can result in conflicts of interest and possible fund mishandling. Grant writing requires significant effort and expertise upfront, so grant writers typically receive compensation through a flat fee or hourly rate rather than a percentage of the grant award.

Myth 4: You Are Too Small to Apply to a Large Grantmaker

It's a common misconception that large grantmakers won't consider new or small applicants. Many seek innovative projects of all sizes. As an individual or small organization, you shouldn't hesitate to apply. Highlight your project's unique value and impact. For example, the Pollination Project (URL: thepollinationproject.org) regularly funds small, grassroots initiatives to create a positive social or environmental impact. By thoroughly researching and aligning with funders' criteria, you can enhance your chances of success, regardless of your size or recognition.

Myth 5: Grants Are "Free Money" With No Strings Attached

Receiving grant funds requires individuals and organizations to uphold specific responsibilities. Grant recipients must submit detailed reports on fund usage and project outcomes. Adherence to these requirements is critical to ensure your good standing and eligibility for future funding opportunities. It's essential to understand the terms of the grant and guarantee that funds are used strictly for the approved purposes.

Myth 6: Grants Are Only for Large Nonprofits

Many think that only large nonprofits with extensive resources can secure grants, but that's false. Individuals and small and medium-sized nonprofits can also win grants by taking a strategic approach. By building strong relationships with funders and demonstrating the impact and need for the funds, smaller organizations can be just as competitive as larger ones. Your involvement in this strategic approach is essential because your efforts in relationship-building and effectively communicating your organization's needs and goals directly influence the success of the grant application.

Myth 7: Once You've Received a Grant, You're Set for Life

Another common misconception is that once you've secured a grant, you'll continue to receive funding indefinitely. In reality, grants are not guaranteed from year to year unless you have been awarded a multi-year grant. Each funding cycle is competitive, and grant seekers must continuously demonstrate their value and impact to secure ongoing support. You must diversify funding sources and not rely solely on grants for long-term sustainability. Your persistence in this effort is critical to maintaining a stable financial base for your initiatives.

Understanding the realities of grant writing and dispelling common myths enables you to approach the process strategically and with an informed mindset. Writing successful grant proposals requires diligence, customization, and strict adherence to funder guidelines, criteria, and expectations. Adhering to these principles boosts your chances of obtaining the essential funds for your initiatives.

Action Items

- To effectively target suitable grants, define your funding needs clearly, whether for operational costs, a specific project, or research.

- Research potential grants using online databases such as Grants.gov, Foundation Center, and corporate websites.

- Check the websites of similar projects to see who funds them, providing insights into potential funders for your project.

- Before applying, review each grant's eligibility criteria, application process, and reporting requirements to ensure you can meet them.

- Reach out to grantmakers directly to clarify questions and establish a relationship, ensuring answers to your inquiries aren't already on their website.

- Understand that large grantmakers often seek innovative projects of all sizes and tailor your proposal to highlight your project's unique value and impact.

- Recognize that grant funds come with specific usage and reporting requirements. Be prepared to maintain detailed financial records and provide progress reports.

- Start your grant writing process early, allowing sufficient time for thorough research and thoughtful responses to detailed questions.

- Diversify your funding sources and do not rely solely on grants for long-term sustainability to ensure ongoing financial stability for your projects.

Before tackling the grant application process, you must deeply understand yourself and your project. In the next chapter, we'll explore how to assess your strengths, define your project's goals, and align them with the right funding opportunities to set yourself up for success.

Chapter 2:

Know Thyself (and Thy Project)

You've got a brilliant idea, and it's about to set the world on fire. But before you light that match, take a moment to reflect. Who are you in this story? What's the narrative that drives you and your project forward? Knowing yourself (and your project) is like finding the right pair of shoes—you won't get far if they don't fit. So, lace up those metaphorical sneakers and sprint toward your goals.

Specifying Your Mission: What Do You Want to Accomplish?

Defining your mission is necessary for successful grant writing. It will articulate your goals clearly and align them with potential funders' priorities. A clear mission ensures that every aspect of your proposal resonates with your organization's core purpose, making it easier for funders to see the value in supporting your work. Here's how to create mission-driven goals that will meet the expectations of potential funders.

Exercises for Defining Your Mission and Vision

- **Mission statement brainstorming session:** You or your organization can brainstorm, starting with research on similar mission statements. List keywords reflecting your core values and goals, identify common themes, and draft multiple mission statements. Refine these into one clear, concise sentence that encapsulates your purpose, ensuring it resonates with who you are and your vision for change.
    - **Example of a mission statement**: "To create vibrant community gardens that promote health, sustainability, and education through collaborative urban gardening." This mission statement captures your purpose,

emphasizing community involvement, sustainability, and the educational aspect of urban gardening, which will be the core values driving your goals.

- **Vision board:** Create a visual vision board representing your goals and aspirations. Include images, words, and phrases that illustrate your vision. This exercise clarifies the change you wish to see in the world and makes sharing and communicating with others easier. You can use the available templates or use a blank layout from Canva (URL: canva.com).

- **The "why" ladder exercise:** Begin with your primary goal and ask yourself "Why?" five times, delving deeper into the purpose behind your mission with each question. This exercise helps you uncover the fundamental reasons driving your project, ensuring your mission statement is rooted in genuine intent. For example, if you want to create community gardens, ask why that's important until you reach the core of your purpose, such as fostering a sense of belonging and promoting environmental stewardship.

- **Elevator pitch practice:** Imagine you're in an elevator with a potential funder and only have 30 seconds to pitch your mission. Write down a few sentences that quickly and compellingly explain what you do and why it matters. Focus on clarity, impact, and your project's unique angle. Then, practice delivering it out loud until it feels natural. This exercise helps you distill your mission into its most potent form, making it easier to communicate your purpose to others.

Now that you've defined your mission, it's time to focus on fine-tuning your project goals and objectives to help you create comprehensive and compelling project proposals that stand out.

Clarifying Your Project Goals and Objectives

When defining your project objectives, it's essential to be specific, measurable, achievable, relevant, and time-bound (SMART). Clear goals provide a roadmap for your project and demonstrate to funders that you have a well-thought-out plan.

- **Specific goals:** Define your goals clearly. For example, instead of saying, "We aim to improve literacy," specify, "We aim to boost reading proficiency by 20% among third graders in our community within one year."

Insider tip: Before you say what you will do, say why you are doing it. For example, "We help immigrant children succeed academically by focusing on boosting reading proficiency."

- **Measurable objectives:** Include metrics to track progress. For instance, "Conduct monthly reading assessments to monitor students' improvement and track progress toward the 20% increase in proficiency."

- **Achievable targets:** Ensure your goals are realistic, given your resources and constraints. If you lack the necessary resources, adjust your goals accordingly. For example, "Host weekly reading sessions and provide each student with one-on-one tutoring, utilizing volunteers and available resources to ensure realistic progress within the given timeframe."

- **Relevant goals:** Be sure your objectives fulfill your or your organization's broader mission. If your mission is to ensure every child receives a good education, your goals should directly contribute to this mission. For instance, "Aligning with our mission to ensure every child receives a good education, this project directly contributes to improving literacy rates among young students in our community."

- **Time-bound:** Set a precise timeline for your goals. This approach will aid in planning and show your commitment to achieving results within a defined period. For example, "Achieve the 20% increase in reading proficiency within one year, with milestones set for quarterly reviews to ensure we are on track."

A goal you have might be to "improve reading levels of students participating in after-school tutoring programs by 50% within six months." This goal is specific, measurable, achievable, mission-focused, and time-bound.

Now that you have a solid understanding of how your goals fulfill your mission, let's move on to the next crucial step: project planning. This section will explore how to turn your goals into fundable projects by creating detailed and actionable plans.

Project Planning: Turning Ideas Into Fundable Projects

Project planning is crucial in turning your ideas into a killer grant proposal. A well-structured project plan provides a clear, actionable roadmap to help you achieve your objectives. Here's how to develop a solid project plan and the tools to assist you.

Steps for Developing a Solid Project Plan

- **SWOT analysis:** Conduct an analysis for strengths, weaknesses, opportunities, and threats (SWOT) to evaluate your internal capabilities and external environment. This strategy will help pinpoint critical areas to emphasize in your narrative and showcase what makes you uniquely positioned for fulfilling your mission. Internal capabilities include resources, skills, and processes, while the external environment covers market trends, competition, and economic conditions.

Note: Appendix B contains an example of a SWOT analysis.

- **Story mapping:** Share the stories of individuals or small organizations you've helped or plan to help. Describe their initial challenges, how your support intervened or intends to intervene, and the positive outcomes or expected impact. This approach gives you the chance to provide emotionally compelling testimonials in your proposal, bringing to life how much your work means in the lives of actual people.

Note: You can refer to Appendix B for an example of story mapping.

- **Gathering perspectives:** Conduct interviews with individuals who have interacted with or benefited from your efforts. This includes talking to any beneficiaries, volunteers, partners, or team members to understand their experiences and views on your work. Collecting these insights helps you build a well-rounded and compelling narrative about your work and impact, which is crucial for crafting a solid mission statement and making your grant applications more persuasive.

- **Develop a detailed project description:** Clearly articulate the urgency and importance of the project by explaining why it matters and needs to happen now. Identify the primary parties involved and define their roles. Detail the methodologies and strategies you will use to achieve the project's objectives, outlining specific activities, goals, and desired outcomes. Determine the project's timeline and location and identify the necessary resources for success. Demonstrate your understanding and commitment to achieving the project goals through a comprehensive and well-planned approach.

Note: Appendix B provides a detailed example of a project description.

- **Create a budget:** Draft a comprehensive budget detailing all anticipated expenses, including direct costs such as salaries, materials, travel, and indirect costs. Ensure each expense is justified and aligns with the scope of your project. A transparent, detailed budget will significantly enhance the strength of your proposal.

Insider tip: Many grant reviewers focus on the budget first. The application won't move to the next round if they find any red flags.

Note: You can refer to Appendix B for an example of a budget.

- **Develop a timeline:** A detailed timeline shows your project's viability. Break your project into phases and assign realistic deadlines to each task. This shows you have a clear plan and helps grant reviewers understand how you will manage and complete the project within the grant period.

Note: You can refer to Appendix B for a timeline sample.

- **Plan for evaluation:** Describe what success looks like for your project, detailing the key outcomes you aim to achieve. Outline an evaluation plan focusing on the specific metrics and methods for measuring this success. This might include surveys, data analysis, or regular progress reports. Your plan should demonstrate what is essential for you to measure to ensure the project's success and impact.

Note: You can refer to Appendix B for a sample of the evaluation plan.

Tools for Project Management and Planning

- **Project management software:** Asana (URL: asana.com), Trello (URL: trello.com), and Monday.com are great tools for handling duties, delegating responsibilities, and tracking improvement. These platforms allow you to instantly complete project boards, establish deadlines, and work with your group.

- **Gantt charts:** Gantt charts effectively display your project timeline. Tools like Microsoft Project (URL: microsoft.com/en-us/microsoft-365/project/project-management-software/) and Smartsheet (URL: smartsheet.com) enable you to create detailed Gantt charts that map out each project phase, making it easier to track milestones and deadlines.

- **Budgeting tools:** Budgeting software, like QuickBooks (URL: quickbooks.intuit.com), designed explicitly for grant budgets, can be used. These tools help you manage and track your expenses, ensuring your financial planning is accurate and transparent.

- **Data collection and analysis tools:** For projects that require extensive data collection, tools like SurveyMonkey (URL: surveymonkey.com) for surveys and SPSS (URL: ibm.com/products/spss-statistics) for data analysis are invaluable. They help you gather, analyze, and present data effectively, supporting your project's objectives with solid evidence.

- **Document management systems:** OneDrive, Dropbox, and Google Drive allow safe document storage and sharing. These platforms ensure your project documents are easily accessible to your team and enable real-time updates.

Developing a solid project plan involves a systematic approach to defining your objectives, conducting research, identifying key personnel, budgeting, creating a timeline, planning for evaluation, and pitching your project. You can streamline this process by leveraging project management tools, ensuring your project is well-organized and on point. A well-crafted and persuasive project plan can significantly improve your likelihood of creating a stellar grant proposal that grant reviewers will gladly fund.

Action Items

- Conduct a brainstorming session to define your mission statement.

- Create a visual picture of your objectives and aspirations by designing a vision board.

- Conduct a SWOT analysis to evaluate your project's internal strengths and weaknesses and the external opportunities and threats that may impact it.

- Gather perspectives through interviews with beneficiaries, volunteers, and partners to enrich your project narrative.

- Develop a detailed project description outlining key objectives, methodologies, and stakeholder roles.

- Draft a comprehensive budget that justifies all anticipated expenses and aligns with the project scope.

- Create a Gantt chart to map your project's timeline, dividing tasks into manageable phases.

- Assign duties, track progress, and work with your group using project management software.

- Outline specific metrics and methods to evaluate your project's success.

- Use document management systems for secure storage, sharing, and real-time updates on project files.

With your solid project plan in place, it's time to identify the ideal funder for your project. It's essential to find the right funding match for success. Let's explore how to research and approach potential funders who align with your mission and goals, ensuring a higher chance of securing support.

Chapter 3:
Finding Your Perfect Match

Like a detective sniffing clues, you're looking for the perfect grant. You've got your list of must-haves, and each grant you come across gets the side-eye. One seems promising, but upon closer inspection, it's more "nice-to-have" than "must-have." Another catches your eye, but the fine print contains red flags. When you're ready to give up, a perfect opportunity appears. It's a match made in grant-writing heaven; you're prepared to make a move.

Grant Hunting: Finding and Choosing the Right Grants

Securing the right grant can take the game to the next level for individuals and small organizations. This step-by-step guide will help you to navigate the grant-hunting process effectively, putting you in control of your funding journey.

Research Available Grant Opportunities

Once you understand your needs and goals, research potential grants using online databases like Grants.gov (URL: grants.gov), Foundation Center (URL: fconline.foundationcenter.org), and GrantStation (URL: grantstation.com). These platforms allow you to search by keyword, funding area, and location to find grants that align with your objectives. For example, search for "grants for Brooklyn community development" if you're seeking funding for a series of free summer Shakespeare plays on the beach in Coney Island.

Leverage Networks and Local Resources

Networking is not just essential; it's a lifeline for finding grants. Connect with colleagues, peers, and nonprofits to uncover potential opportunities. Attend events and conferences to meet grantmakers and other funding organizations. Also, explore local foundations and government grants often supporting community-based initiatives, such as the Brooklyn Arts Council (URL: brooklynartscouncil.org) or the NYC Department of Cultural Affairs (URL: nyc.gov/site/dcla/index.page), which might fund your Shakespeare performances on Coney Island beach. Local government websites like NYC.gov (URL: nyc.gov/site/dcla/cultural-funding/cultural-funding.page) or LAcity.gov (URL: culture.lacity.gov/grants/cultural-grant-program-org) often provide listings of grants available for small businesses and nonprofits. Building a grassroots support network within the community can make the grant search process less overwhelming and more manageable.

Evaluate Grant Opportunities

After you compile a list of potential grants, assess them to identify the best matches. Consider these key factors:

- **Eligibility criteria:** Ensure that you or your organization meets all eligibility requirements, including the specific geographic area, organization size, experience level, budget range, and any necessary matching funds.

- **Alignment with goals:** Ensure the grant matches you and your organization's vision and goals.

- **Funding amount and duration:** Assess if the funding amount and duration are sufficient for your project.

- **Reporting requirements:** Ensure you and your organization can meet the reporting requirements. For example, suppose a grant requires data collection and analysis, requiring you to hire consultants. You and your organization may need more resources to manage it. In that case, looking for a better fit may be wiser.

Networking Like a Pro: Developing Solid Relationships With Funders

Networking is another objective for anyone looking to secure funding, whether you're an individual seeking grants or a small organization aiming to grow. Building relationships with funders requires a strategic approach that combines effective communication, persistence, and a genuine interest in the funders' goals and missions. Trust and confidence are at the core of these relationships—funders must trust you to honor their investment and feel confident in your ability to execute the project successfully. Demonstrating reliability and a clear plan for success is essential to fostering this trust and securing long-term partnerships.

Insider tip: Truly savvy grant seekers overdeliver in these areas. If you are a trustworthy grantee, funders will recommend you to other funders—believe me, this does happen!

Tips for Effective Networking and Relationship-Building

Do Your Homework

When networking, thorough research is essential. Understand a funder's priorities, past projects, and mission before reaching out. This strategy helps tailor your pitch to show alignment with their goals.

Insider tip: Dig a little deeper to find out what they are genuinely passionate about and add additional value.

For example, if a foundation focuses on educational initiatives and targets teenage girls, emphasize how your project can dramatically improve their self-esteem through improved academic outcomes. Funders prefer applicants who clearly understand their objectives and past initiatives. Aligning your project with the funder's mission boosts your likelihood of getting the grant by demonstrating your shared dedication to their cause, which can lead to a more significant and long-term relationship.

Attend Relevant Events

Fundraising events, industry conferences, and webinars present exceptional opportunities to connect with likely funders. You can learn from experts and introduce your project by attending these events. Focus on formal presentations and informal interactions during breaks, as these can be equally valuable.

Insider tip: Funders often attend events (openings, ribbon cuttings, and award ceremonies) to see who else is doing exciting work. Remember, funders look for great people and projects.

Leverage Social Media

Use specialized forums, X (formerly Twitter; URL: x.com), and LinkedIn (URL: linkedin.com) to connect with funders and stay updated on their activities. Follow and engage with their content on other platforms, such as Instagram (URL: instagram.com), sharing your insights on relevant topics. This online presence keeps you on their radar and shows you are confident, dedicated, and transparent in your work.

Follow Up

Send a thank-you email or message after an initial meeting or interaction. This brilliant, overlooked gesture can leave an ongoing impression and encourage further communication. Referencing your previous conversation shows that you value their time and insights. Funders appreciate applicants who are courteous and proactive in maintaining communication.

Provide Regular Updates

Another goal is to update funders on your progress regularly. Share updates on your project regularly, highlighting both achievements and challenges. This honesty cultivates trust and displays your commitment to the integrity of your project. Funders value consistent updates and feel more connected to projects that maintain ongoing communication.

Seek Feedback

Seek feedback on your work to gain valuable insights from funders. Their suggestions can enhance your project's chances of success and potential future funding. Showing a willingness to learn and adapt strengthens your relationship with funders and demonstrates your shared commitment.

How to Communicate With Funders

- **Be clear and concise:** Clear communication with funders is essential. Make sure your emails, proposals, and conversations are concise and direct. Use simple language and emphasize the main message.

- **Personalize your communication:** Funders, like most people, don't appreciate generic messages. Therefore, personalize your emails and proposals by addressing the funder by name and emphasizing specific aspects of their work that align with your project. Always be courteous, appreciative, and concise by personalizing your emails and proposals and highlighting particular elements of their work that resonate with your project.

Ready to enhance your grant-seeking efforts? Let's explore the essential tools of the trade. Next, we'll discuss digital resources and grant databases that can streamline your search for funding opportunities best suited for your project.

Tools of the Trade: Digital Resources and Grant Databases

Leveraging digital tools and grant databases can significantly improve your success in identifying the proper grants for yourself or your organization. By effectively utilizing these resources, you can streamline your grant research and application process, ensuring you find the most suitable funding opportunities for your needs. Here's an overview of valuable tools and databases as well as tips on leveraging technology for success in grant writing.

Overview of Useful Tools and Databases

- **Grants.gov (URL: grants.gov):** This platform is the primary resource for federal grants in the United States, offering a detailed database of funding opportunities across multiple sectors. It enables you to filter searches by keyword, funding type, eligibility, and more, facilitating the search for grants that match your organization's mission. Additionally, you can create an account to obtain information about new grant prospects.

- **Foundation Directory Online (FDO; URL: fconline.foundationcenter.org):** Candid's Foundation Directory Online is an excellent tool for locating foundation grants. It offers comprehensive profiles of funders, detailing their past recipients, funding priorities, and contact information. This resource streamlines recognizing and connecting with foundations likely to support your projects.

- **GrantStation (URL: grantstation.com):** Ideal for national and international funding searches, GrantStation offers a user-friendly interface with keyword searching, proposal writing assistance, and various research tools. It's particularly beneficial for smaller nonprofits seeking a wide range of funding opportunities without extensive resources.

- **GrantWatch (URL: grantwatch.com):** This database helps find grants from various sectors, including nonprofit, government, and small business grants. It provides detailed information on each grant, including eligibility requirements and application deadlines, which can save you time during the research phase.

- **GrantGopher (URL: grantgopher.com):** GrantGopher, designed for small nonprofits, is celebrated for its simplicity and affordability. It provides essential search functions, alerts, and notifications for new grant opportunities. This budget-friendly tool offers a low-cost subscription plan that accommodates smaller organizations.

- **Artist Grant (URL: artistgrant.org):** This specialized database is perfect for individual artists seeking funding. It features a curated list of grants, fellowships, and residencies specifically tailored to the needs of visual artists, writers, and other creative professionals. The platform provides insights into deadlines, eligibility, and application requirements, helping artists find and secure the funding they need.

- **Scholarships.com (URL: scholarships.com):** While primarily known for academic scholarships, this database also includes various grant opportunities for individuals, particularly in education and research. It allows users to filter searches based on their field of study, background, and interests, making finding grants that align with their personal goals easier.

How to Leverage Technology for Grant Writing Success

- **Create a detailed grant calendar:** Use digital tools like GrantStation's calendar function to track application deadlines, reporting requirements, and critical dates. This approach ensures you efficiently manage multiple grant applications and always meet essential deadlines.

- **Utilize keyword search and filters:** Most grant databases feature robust search functions, enabling you to filter by specific criteria like grant type, eligible organizations, location, and funding priorities. By honing your search parameters, you can swiftly pinpoint the most relevant grants for you or your organization, thereby saving time in building a list of targeted funders.

- **Set up alerts and notifications:** Grants.gov and GrantStation include features that alert you to new grant opportunities that match your saved searches. This proactive strategy keeps you informed about potential funding sources without the need to monitor databases constantly.

- **Leverage proposal writing tools:** Many grant databases provide resources and templates for writing practical grant proposals. These tools can guide you through the process, ensuring you include all necessary information and present your organization in the best light. Some platforms, like GrantStation, offer webinars and expert advice to enhance your grant writing skills.

- **Research funders thoroughly:** Use databases like Foundation Directory Online (URL: fconline.foundationcenter.org) to gather detailed information about potential funders. Understanding a funder's past giving patterns, funding priorities, and application preferences can help you tailor your proposal to their interests, increasing your likelihood of receiving funding.

Examples of Success

A small nonprofit focusing on after-school programs: Using GrantGopher's simple search tools and affordable subscription plan, the organization identified and applied for several small grants tailored to educational initiatives, ultimately securing funding for their new literacy program.

A grassroots environmental organization: Leveraging the detailed profiles and search functionalities of the Foundation Directory Online, the organization identified foundations with a history of supporting conservation projects. By tailoring their proposals to align with these funders' priorities, they successfully secured multiple grants to expand their conservation efforts.

A freelance artist seeking funding for a community mural project: Using the streamlined search options and grant alerts from GrantWatch, the artist discovered a local arts grant designed explicitly for public art initiatives. With a well-crafted proposal highlighting the mural's potential impact on the community, the artist secured the grant, allowing the project to bring vibrant, culturally significant artwork to a previously underutilized public space.

Utilizing digital resources and grant databases improves the efficiency and focus of your grant writing process. This strategic approach saves time and significantly boosts your chances of zeroing in on the best grants you or your organization needs to thrive.

Action Items

- Define your organization's specific needs and goals before starting your grant search to target your efforts effectively.

- Use online databases to search for organizations that can provide grants for your project.

- Create a comprehensive grant calendar to track application deadlines, reporting requirements, and other essential dates.

- Connect with peers and attend relevant events to show that you are supportive and active in discovering grant opportunities and engaging with potential funders.

- Use social media to stay updated on funders' activities and engage with their content, showcasing your work.

Now that you understand where to find grants and how to select the best ones, it's time to focus on the critical steps in the next chapter. Thorough research and meticulous preparation are essential for crafting successful grant applications and ensuring your proposals are compelling and well-supported. Let's delve into these vital steps in detail.

Chapter 4:

Research and Preparation

Imagine you're about to bake the perfect cake without reading the recipe—sounds risky, right? The same goes for grant writing. Research and preparation are essential ingredients, ensuring your proposal rises to the occasion and impresses the funders. Dive in, gather your facts, and set the stage for success!

Understanding Grant Guidelines: Reading Between the Lines

Understanding grant guidelines is necessary when you're writing grants. You must read between the lines to understand the change in the world the funder wishes to see and ensure your proposal aligns perfectly with their strategic objectives. Let's break down how to decode these guidelines and position yourself as the best candidate for the grant.

Decoding and Interpreting Grant Guidelines

Grant guidelines can often feel like a foreign language, filled with jargon and specific requirements that can be daunting. However, they are essentially a blueprint for what the funder seeks. Here's how you can decode them:

- **Identify key requirements:** Highlight essential elements like deadlines, funding priorities, and eligibility criteria. Funders clearly and structurally outline what they seek, such as projects addressing environmental sustainability or supporting underserved communities.
    - **Example:** A local foundation's guideline states, "We prioritize funding for projects that enhance educational opportunities for underprivileged children in urban areas." This tells you that your proposal should focus

on educational initiatives explicitly targeting this demographic.

- **Understand the funders' goals:** Funders have specific objectives they desire to accomplish through their grants. You can adjust your proposal to meet these goals when you understand them. Research the funder's past grants, annual reports, and mission statements to understand their priorities.

    - **Example:** If corporate philanthropy has a history of funding science, technology, engineering, and mathematics (STEM) education programs, and your project involves setting up a tech lab in a school, highlight how your initiative uniquely aligns with their commitment to STEM education.

- **Look for explicit instructions:** Many grant guidelines provide clear instructions on what to include in your proposal, such as project narratives, budgets, and evaluation plans. By following these instructions precisely, you demonstrate thoroughness and attention to detail.

    - **Example:** Government agencies always require a detailed budget with specific line items for personnel, equipment, and administrative costs. It's essential to provide clear budget notes to assure funders you can manage their investment effectively.

- **Pay attention to formatting requirements:** Funders often specify formatting requirements, such as font size, page limits, and section headings. Ignoring these can lower your ranking.

    - **Example:** A foundation specifies that proposals be no more than 10 pages, use 12-point Times New Roman font, and include sections titled "Project Summary," "Objectives," and "Budget." Adhering to these policies is critical for demonstrating professionalism and respect for the funder's process.

Tips for Ensuring Compliance With Funder Requirements

To ensure your application is accepted, you must meet funder requirements. Here are some recommendations to help you stay on track:

- **Create a checklist:** Use the grant guidelines to create a checklist that includes all critical components. This includes eligibility criteria, required documents, formatting specifications, and submission deadlines.

    - **Example:** You can find the Grant Application Checklist Template under Appendix C.

- **Seek clarification:** If you have policy questions, contact the funder. Most funders appreciate applicants who take the initiative to understand their requirements fully.

    - **Example:** If you're unsure about the scope of eligible expenses, contact the grant administrator and ask, "Can travel expenses for project staff be included in the budget?" This will confirm you're on the right track and can prevent costly mistakes.

- **Review and proofread:** Review your proposal before submitting it to ensure it follows all guidelines. Have someone else proofread it; they may catch errors you've overlooked.

    - **Example:** A colleague might notice that you've exceeded the page limit or missed a required section, allowing you to make necessary adjustments before submission.

- **Use templates and samples**: If available, utilize templates and samples provided by the funder. These can offer valuable insights into the structure and tone preferred by the funder.

    - **Example:** If the funder provides a sample budget template, use it as a guide to structure your budget according to their expectations.

Real-World Success: Before-and-After Examples

Consider the case of a small nonprofit seeking funding for an after-school program. Initially, its proposal was vague and lacked alignment with the funder's priorities. After revisiting the grant guidelines and focusing on specific instructions, the nonprofit revised its proposal to highlight how its program would improve educational outcomes for low-income students, directly addressing the funder's goals. This targeted approach led to a successful grant award.

Another organization applied for a grant to expand a community garden but faced rejection due to an unclear budget and vague objectives. After carefully reviewing the funder's guidelines, they included detailed budget items and specific, achievable goals in their revised proposal, successfully securing the needed funding.

Next, consider the story of an individual artist seeking a grant to fund a public art installation. Their proposal initially lacked a clear connection between the project's impact and the funder's mission to promote community engagement through the arts. After receiving feedback and carefully studying the funder's priorities, the artist revised the proposal to articulate how the installation would foster community interaction and reflect local culture. By including specific examples of how the project would engage different community groups and providing a detailed project timeline, the artist successfully secured the grant, allowing the installation to become a reality.

To succeed in grant writing:

1. Be sure you clearly understand the funder's requirements. Adhering to grant guidelines and meeting all requirements will boost your chances of success.

2. To ensure your project stands out among applicants, see to it that your proposal adds distinct value to the people your funder cares about.

3. Equip yourself with the knowledge and tools to meet these challenges head-on, and you'll be well on your way to securing the funding you need to bring your vision to life.

The Art of Research: Know Your Funder and Their Priorities

Understanding your funder is crucial in grant writing. Focus on learning what your funders care about and aligning your project with their priorities. Think of it as a matchmaking process—you want to find the perfect match that will make your project shine in their eyes.

Techniques for Researching Funders

- **Review funders' websites:** Visit the funders' websites to understand their mission, values, and previously funded projects. Most foundations have detailed sections on their funding priorities and often share success stories, giving you a clear picture of what they seek and who they have funded. For example, the Ford Foundation's website (URL: fordfoundation.org) offers a comprehensive list of grantees, showcasing its commitment to social justice and equity across various sectors.

- **Analyze annual reports:** Annual reports can be gold mines of information. They often include detailed descriptions of funded projects, financial statements, and messages from key leaders about future directions. Reviewing these reports lets you gauge a funder's priorities and strategic goals.

- **Network with peers:** Talk to colleagues and peers who have successfully secured grants. They can share their personal experiences and tips on what specific funders look for and how to tailor your proposal. Networking events, workshops, and webinars can help you connect and gain insights.

- **Study funded projects:** Review past projects funded by the organization by visiting its website or conducting a quick search. For example, if a foundation supports community gardens, examine the size, scope, and impact of its financed gardens.

- **Engage with funders:** Ensure you understand the funder's preferred contact method before reaching out. Funders may offer information sessions or office hours and have program officers designated to speak with potential grantees.

Case Studies of Successful Research Strategies

Case Study 1: Small Nonprofit Securing a Major Foundation Grant

A small nonprofit focused on youth education wanted to expand its after-school programs. It targeted the Walton Family Foundation, known for its investment in education. The nonprofit extensively researched the foundation's priorities and mission values using the techniques mentioned above. It discovered that the foundation was particularly interested in projects that showed measurable outcomes in student performance.

The nonprofit attended several webinars hosted by the foundation, networked with other grantees, and reviewed annual reports to understand the foundation's strategic goals. They also reached out to a program officer for an informational meeting. This thorough research allowed them to tailor their proposal to highlight how their program's outcomes aligned with the foundation's goals. Their efforts paid off with a substantial grant that doubled their program's capacity.

Case Study 2: Community Group Launching a Local Food Pantry

A grassroots community group wanted to start a local food bank and identified potential funders such as local businesses, national foundations, and government grants. They researched these funders' websites and annual reports, discovering that a local corporate philanthropy organization, which had previously supported several community initiatives, now focused on food security.

They attended a community networking event where they met representatives from the local corporate philanthropy organization. These interactions provided invaluable insights into what the funder valued most—community impact and volunteer involvement. Using this information, the group tailored their grant application to emphasize their solid volunteer base and the immediate impact the food bank would have on local food security. This well-researched approach led to a successful grant application and the launch of their food bank.

Researching prospective funders and embracing their priorities will enhance your likelihood of acquiring grants. Finding the right match and crafting a proposal that aligns with what the funder values most will position you as the best candidate for the grant. Dive into this process with curiosity and diligence, and you'll set yourself as a successful grant winner.

Gathering Your Team: Who You Need and Why

When tackling the grant writing process, assembling the right team is essential. Whether part of a small organization or flying solo, understanding the key roles and responsibilities can make the journey smoother and more successful. Let's break down who you need on your grant writing team and why they're essential.

Identifying Key Team Members for Grant Writing

- **The Visionary (Project Leader)**
    - **Role:** This person sees the big picture. They know the project's goals, objectives, and desired outcomes. They can passionately articulate why the project matters.
    - **Why:** The Visionary keeps the team aligned with the project's mission and ensures the proposal stays true to the organization's values and goals.
- **The Researcher**
    - **Role:** This person digs deep into the details. They identify potential grant opportunities, understand

funder priorities, and gather the necessary data to support the proposal.

- **Why:** Conducting accurate and thorough research boosts your chances of finding the proper grants and aligning your proposal with the funder's expectations.

- **The Writer**

  - **Role:** This individual crafts the narrative of the grant proposal. They are skilled at telling your story compellingly and clearly, ensuring the language is clear, persuasive, and engaging.

  - **Why:** Crafting a well-written proposal is essential for grabbing the funder's attention and communicating the significance of your project.

- **The Number Cruncher (Budget Specialist)**

  - **Role:** This person is responsible for creating the budget and ensuring that all financial aspects of the project are accurately represented and justified.

  - **Why:** Funders need to see a realistic and well-thought-out budget. It demonstrates that you've planned your project thoroughly and can be trusted to manage funds responsibly.

- **The Proofreader**

  - **Role:** This team member reviews the proposal to find any errors or inconsistencies, ensuring the document is polished and professional.

  - **Why:** Minor mistakes can easily undermine the credibility of your proposal. A clean, error-free document reflects your organization's attention to detail and professionalism.

Roles and Responsibilities in the Grant Writing Process

In smaller organizations or for those new to grant writing, one person often needs to juggle multiple roles. For example, suppose you're both a Visionary and a Writer. In that case, you can effectively leverage your deep understanding of the project to convey its significance in your proposal. Managing both Researcher and Number Cruncher is also feasible—use online tools and templates to help with research and budgeting. To ensure accuracy and clarity, have someone else proofread your work or take a break before proofreading it yourself to catch any overlooked mistakes.

For example, if you're passionate about launching a neighborhood garden, you might divide the process into the following roles:

- **Visionary/Writer:** Describe the community garden's educational, emotional, and environmental benefits.

- **Researcher/Number Cruncher:** Identify relevant grants, gather data on similar projects, and draft a budget for necessary supplies and workshops.

- **Proofreader:** Request a review from a friend or colleague to polish your proposal.

When you understand and embrace these roles, you'll be well-prepared to tackle the grant writing process, whether part of a small team or working solo. Each role is crucial to the strength and success of your proposal.

Action Items

- Identify potential grants that match your project's mission and needs.

- Collect the essential data and information to support your proposal, concentrating on funder priorities and past successful grants.

- Follow all formatting and submission guidelines the funder provides, including font size, page limits, and required sections.

- Use the grant guidelines to create a checklist that ensures you include all necessary details.

- If any guidelines are vague, ask the funder for further details to ensure your application meets all the requirements.

- Use templates and samples provided by the funder to structure your proposal to align with their expectations.

After completing your grant research and preparation, the next step is to create a captivating narrative. In the upcoming chapter, "Writing with Style," you'll learn how to present your proposal with clarity and impact, ensuring your ideas resonate with funders and set your application apart.

Chapter 5:

Writing With Style (and Substance)

As a grant writer, your wordsmithing skills will play a vital role in the funding game. Your ability to craft compelling proposals that get funded depends on how well you can tell your story of innovation and impact. Your writing may mesmerize readers and ultimately hold their attention. But let's face it: While your poetic prowess may be impressive, style must serve substance. A well-structured proposal with a clear flow can be as powerful as your literary gems. Let's dive into the nuts and bolts of proposal writing basics: structure and flow.

Proposal Writing Basics: Structure and Flow

Writing a successful grant proposal involves understanding its essential components and organizing them to create a persuasive and coherent document. Mastering these basics can significantly increase an individual's or small organization's chances of securing funding. More importantly, it can pave the way for transformative projects that can change lives and communities.

Standard Components of a Grant Proposal

A comprehensive grant proposal includes several essential sections, each serving a specific purpose.

- **Project synopsis:** This section gives a brief overview of your proposal. Ensure it is concise yet compelling, encapsulating the core of your proposal in just two or three sentences.

- **Introduction:** Introduce your organization, describe its mission and history, and explain why it is well-suited to execute the proposed project successfully. This section builds your credibility and sets the entire proposal's context.

- **Problem statement:** A problem statement outlines the specific issue or challenge your project aims to address, supported by data and research to validate its importance. In contrast, a needs statement is broader, describing the general needs or gaps within a community or target group, often serving as the foundation for identifying the problem. For example, suppose you are seeking funding for an after-school program. In that case, the problem statement might focus on the lack of safe, productive activities for local youth, highlighting statistics on the high rates of juvenile delinquency during after-school hours. Meanwhile, the needs statement would discuss the lack of accessible programs that engage and support youth in the community.

Insider tip: Instead of presenting a problem for a funder to solve, offer them an opportunity to drive change. This way, they create a positive impact rather than simply fill a gap. Achieve this by addressing *why*, *why now*, and *who* before outlining the *what*. If a funder finds the project compelling and appealing, they will be enthusiastic about providing financial support. This principle is critical in successful grant proposals.

- **Project description:** This section is the heart of your proposal. Outline your project in detail, including objectives, methods, and activities. Summarize your actions, detail the strategies you will employ, and specify the timeline for completing each step. Here's a detailed project description:
    - **Example of a Youth Soccer Skills Development Program:**
        - **Why:** Our community faces a rising need for youth engagement due to increasing dropout rates and juvenile delinquency. This project aims to provide a positive environment that fosters skill development and personal growth.
        - **Why now:** With current academic performance declining and extracurricular activities dwindling, immediate intervention is crucial to prevent

further adverse outcomes and to set our youth on a positive path.

- **Who:** The project will target at-risk youth aged 12-17 within the community, involving local educators, volunteers, and parents as key stakeholders.

- **What:** We will implement an after-school soccer program to build teamwork, discipline, and leadership skills. The curriculum includes soccer drills, life skills workshops, and mentorship sessions.

- **When:** The program will run for 12 weeks, starting in September, with sessions held thrice a week after school.

- **Where:** All activities will occur at the community center and local soccer fields, providing a safe and accessible location for participants.

This approach ensures that the project is timely, relevant, and designed to make a meaningful impact on the community.

- **Goals and objectives:** Define your project's goals and the specific, measurable objectives to help you achieve them. Goals are broad outcomes, while objectives are concrete steps you will take. For instance, your goal might be to improve community health by increasing access to nutritious food. An objective to support this goal could be establishing three community gardens within the next 12 months to provide fresh produce to residents.

- **Evaluation plan:** You'll use qualitative and quantitative methods to gauge the project's success. You will conduct pre- and post-program surveys, track academic performance, and perform participant interviews to assess the impact. This method thoroughly evaluates the project's success and highlights areas for improvement.

Note: Please check Appendix D for an example of an evaluation form.

- **Budget:** Create a detailed budget that lists all projected expenses and revenue. Describe each line item to clarify fund usage. Ensure accuracy and transparency so that funders fully understand the allocation of their money.

Note: Please check Appendix B for examples of poorly written and well-written budgets.

- **Sustainability plan:** You should explain how to sustain the project after the grant term concludes. This may include strategies for future funding, establishing partnerships, or garnering community support.

- **Appendices:** Include supplementary materials that boost your proposal, such as financial reports, testimonials, resumes of key staff, and letters of support.

Note: You can find letters of support templates here: grantboost.io/blog/Letters-of-Support/#letters-of-support-for-grants-templates/.

You can also find a sample of a letter of support under Appendix E or at the Albion College website (URL: albion.edu/wp-content/uploads/2021/11/Sample_Letter-of-Support.pdf).

Organizing Your Proposal for Maximum Impact

To ensure your proposal stands out, follow these organizational tips:

- **Answer questions directly:** Respond concisely without additional context or elaboration.

Insider tip: Start each answer by rephrasing the question to keep your response focused and clear. For example, how will your program support the growth of young soccer players? Our program will support the growth of young soccer players by providing specialized coaching.

- **Include supporting materials:** Clearly label testimonials, photos, and references; attach them or include them in an appendix.

- **Use bullet points:** To make key points memorable, highlight them with bullet points followed by concise, descriptive sentences.

- **Utilize white space:** Break up text to make it visually appealing and easier for grant reviewers to read.

- **Label and cue work samples:** Ensure videos, recordings, or other samples are clearly labeled, properly cued, and listed for easy access.

Adhering to these guidelines can help you craft a well-structured and impactful grant proposal that best presents you as the best candidate for the grant and boosts your chances of getting a "yes."

With your proposal's structure and flow established, the next crucial step is to craft a narrative that emotionally engages funders. Telling a well-crafted story can significantly enhance the effectiveness of your proposal. Learn how to vividly depict your project and connect emotionally with grant reviewers through expert storytelling techniques in grant writing.

Composing a Persuasive Narrative: Storytelling in Grant Writing

Storytelling enhances grant proposals by turning them into engaging narratives that resonate emotionally with funders. This technique lets you convey your project's importance, potential impact, and commitment to the cause.

Techniques for Engaging Storytelling

Start With a Strong Hook

Begin your narrative with a compelling emotional hook that instantly engages the reader. Use a surprising fact, a moving story, or a challenging question. For example, when writing a grant for a community literacy program, you might begin with, "Picture a child who dreams of reading but lacks access to books."

Develop a Clear and Compelling Character

People connect with people, not just abstract concepts. Introduce a protagonist who represents the individuals or communities your project will benefit. Describe their struggles, hopes, and transformations. For example, "Meet Sarah, a single mother of three who has always wanted to read to her children but never learned how."

Establish the Setting

Set the scene to provide context. Where is your story taking place? What are the conditions? Answering these questions helps the funder visualize the environment and understand the urgency of your project. For example, "In the heart of our city's underfunded neighborhoods, children like Sarah's kids lack access to basic educational resources."

Highlight the Conflict

Every compelling story involves a conflict or challenge that needs addressing. This is where you explain the problem your project seeks to resolve. Support your points with data and statistics. For instance, "Over 60% of children in our community are reading below their grade level, and this gap keeps growing without intervention. Without immediate action, these children face a high risk of never graduating high school, limiting their opportunities for college and trapping them in a cycle of poverty."

Show the Journey and Solution

Outline your protagonist's challenges, stakes, and journey and how your project will help them achieve their goals. Describe your methods and outline steps to make this vital change in their lives. For example, "Our literacy program provides one-on-one tutoring, free books, and parent literacy workshops to bridge the educational disparity and nurture self-confidence and a love of reading."

Conclude With a Vision of the Future

Envision a future where your project allows people to thrive, creating lasting positive change and empowering the community. Here's an example: "With your support, we can ensure that children like Sarah's kids not only learn to read but also thrive academically and personally, breaking the cycle of illiteracy."

Examples of Compelling Narratives

- **Community garden initiative:** "Envision a community where empty lots turn into thriving gardens. Maria, a resident, used to buy her vegetables from a distant grocery store. Now she picks fresh produce from the garden she helped cultivate. Our project will empower more residents like Maria to realize they have the power to make changes in the world, fostering community spirit and healthy living."

- **Youth mentorship program:** "Jake, a teenager from a troubled home, struggled in school and faced an uncertain future. Through our mentorship program, Jake found a mentor who guided him through high school and inspired him to pursue a college degree. We aim to replicate Jake's success story for hundreds of at-risk youth in our city."

These narratives are about presenting facts and making funders feel connected to your cause and motivated to support your work.

Composing a convincing narrative is only one part of successful grant writing. Equally important is ensuring your proposal is explicit and straightforward. By avoiding jargon and overly complex language, you can make your grant proposal accessible and understandable to all potential funders, regardless of their background knowledge. Let's explore how to keep your writing straightforward and impactful.

Simplifying Your Language: Clear and Concise Communication

Suggestions for Straightforward and Succinct Writing

Grant writing for individuals and small organizations is an art that demands clarity and brevity. Funders often review numerous proposals, so making yours stand out with clear and concise writing is essential. Here is some advice to assist you:

- **Be familiar with the terms and language:** Understand the specific terms and language funders use so you can effectively communicate your project's value. This technique boosts your proposal's credibility and aligns it with the funder's priorities.

- **Outline your proposal:** Start with a well-structured outline to organize your thoughts effectively, ensuring you address all critical aspects of your project. These elements are fundamental:
    - a straightforward introduction
    - a compelling needs statement
    - specific objectives
    - thorough methods for achieving your objectives
    - a detailed timeline outlining key milestones and deadlines
    - an evaluation plan
    - a comprehensive budget

- **Use simple language:** Avoid complex terminology and specialized language. Select clear, simple words that everyone can understand. For example, say "use" rather than "utilize."

- **Be specific and concrete:** Incorporate detailed information and specific examples, using quantifiable data like numbers and measurable outcomes to bolster your arguments. This well-supported approach not only enhances clearness but also strengthens the quality of your proposal.

- **Edit ruthlessly:** After drafting your proposal, revise it critically. Remove unnecessary words and redundancies. Streamline sentences to convey information concisely. Reading your proposal aloud can help identify convoluted areas that need simplification.

- **Seek feedback:** Get feedback from colleagues, mentors, or professionals in the field. They can offer new insights and point out areas that need improvement. Constructive criticism is invaluable in refining your grant proposal.

Familiar Jargon Pitfalls and How to Avoid Them

Jargon in your grant proposal can confuse your readers and disconnect them from your message. Here are common mistakes and how you can avoid them.

- **Technical terms:** Using industry-specific language can confuse reviewers with different background knowledge. Simplify technical terms or provide brief explanations when necessary. For example, instead of saying "synergize operational frameworks," say "work together efficiently."

- **Acronym:** Using too many acronyms can make your proposal challenging to follow. Spell out the entire phrase when you first use it and follow it with the abbreviation in parentheses. For example, write "Non-Governmental Organization (NGO)."

- **Buzzwords:** Avoid trendy buzzwords that lack substance. Words like "disruptive innovation" or "paradigm shift" can be vague and overused. Instead, describe what you mean in plain language. For example, instead of "disruptive innovation," you could say "a new approach that greatly changes current practices."

- **Passive voice:** Using passive voice often lengthens sentences and reduces clarity. Opt for an active voice to enhance transparency and engagement in your writing. For example, instead of "The project will be managed by the team," write "The team will manage the project."

- **Complex sentences:** Long, complex sentences can take time to understand. Improve readability by breaking complex sentences into shorter, clearer ones. For instance, rather than writing, "In order to achieve sustainable environmental practices, the project will implement a series of innovative strategies that leverage community engagement," simplify it to, "The project will use innovative strategies and involve the community to achieve sustainable environmental practices."

By avoiding these pitfalls and following the tips for clear and concise writing, your grant proposals will be more approachable and stand a better chance of impressing grant reviewers. Making a compelling case for your project relies on clarity and brevity. If possible, consider reviewing successful grant applications.

Tips on Presenting Yourself or Your Organization Compellingly

- **Know your audience:** Understand the funder's mission and values and target beneficiaries to craft your story that resonates with their passion and the change they want to create. Align your proposal with the funder's priorities to prove you're the perfect candidate for the grant. Study the funder's previous grants to grasp their preferences and expectations.

- **Humanize your narrative:** Focus on who will benefit from your project. Talk about people and their individual stories to make the problem and your solutions more tangible. Specific and emotional stories evoke empathy and help grant reviewers connect deeply with your cause. Share how your initiative transformed the life of a particular child instead of just stating that your program helps underprivileged children.

- **Be the guide, not the hero:** Position yourself and your organization as the agents of change, helping the real heroes—your beneficiaries—overcome their challenges. This strategy makes your proposal more emotionally engaging. It establishes you and your organization as compassionate collaborators who achieve successful results. Think of classic storylines where the guide (like Gandalf or Yoda) plays a crucial role in making life better for others.

- **Use clear and convincing language:** Use simple language to make your message clear and emphasize the significance of your work. This approach ensures that reviewers easily grasp and support your project.

Insider tip: Never use words that make a grant reviewer feel stupid or have to stop and look it up.

- **Showcase your impact:** Showcase your programs' impact using data and testimonials. Highlight your success with statistics, case studies, and feedback from those you've assisted. For instance, if you operate a tutoring program, share improvements in students' grades and include quotes from parents and teachers to illustrate how the program changed their lives. The more emotional the impact, the better.

Action Items

- Know the funder's mission and priorities so you can tailor your proposal accordingly.

- Create a well-structured checklist including all critical sections like the project description, introduction, and needs statement.

- Write so all readers can easily understand your content.

- Provide concrete examples and specific details to enhance your assertions and show your proposal's human impact.

- Avoid using industry-specific acronyms excessively; spell them out on first use to ensure understanding.

- Use active voice to make your proposal more explicit and more enjoyable.

Now that you understand the importance of clear and concise writing, it's time to dive deeper into the core components of grant writing. In this chapter, you'll learn how to structure each proposal section, from the executive summary to the sustainability plan, ensuring your project stands out and secures funding.

Chapter 6:

The Core Components

Imagine piecing together a jigsaw puzzle. Begin with the corner pieces—those essential elements that anchor the whole picture. In grant writing, these corner pieces are your core components. You've nailed down your vision, mission, and goals; you're building a masterpiece. But wait—there's a gap in the picture. What's missing? Ah, yes, the crucial piece that shows why this project matters is the statement of need. Without it, your puzzle is incomplete, leaving reviewers scratching their heads and wondering, *Why am I reading this?* Now, let's dive into defining the need and crafting a compelling statement of need that propels your grant proposal.

Statement of Need: Defining the Need

When crafting a problem statement, you're not just describing an issue but setting the stage for why your project is vital. Think of it as the cornerstone of your grant proposal—it needs to be solid, clear, and compelling. To articulate the problem your project addresses, focus on specifics. Don't just say, "There's a lack of resources for after-school programs." Instead, dig more deeply: "In our community, 65% of low-income families have no access to affordable after-school programs, leading to an increase in juvenile delinquency and a decline in academic performance."

Support your claims with data and research. For example, when writing for a small organization seeking funding for mental health services, you could emphasize that "The National Alliance on Mental Illness reports that one in five adults experiences mental illness, but only 47% receive treatment (*Mental Health*, 2023)." This technique demonstrates the urgent need for your project.

You can find solid examples of needs statements in successful grants. Take, for example, a community food pantry seeking funds: "In our county, 20% of children live in food-insecure households, leading to malnutrition and poor academic performance. Without intervention, these children are at a higher risk of chronic health issues." This statement is powerful because it's specific, backed by data, and paints a vivid human picture of the problem.

Your statement of need should resonate with the grant reviewers, making them see the urgency and importance of your project. They should immediately understand why your work matters and compel them to recommend it for funding.

After identifying the problem, you can focus on your goal. Let's explore how to outline your goals and objectives clearly, setting the path for your project's success.

Purposes and Goals: What You Strive to Accomplish

You need to know your destination before you can chart your course, and setting clear goals and objectives is the key to doing that. When writing a grant proposal, this step is non-negotiable. To reach your goals, set SMART objectives: specific, measurable, achievable, relevant, and time-bound steps that will guide you toward those outcomes.

For example, instead of saying, "We aim to improve literacy rates," you'd say, "We will increase reading proficiency by 20% among 100 elementary school students within two years by implementing a weekly after-school reading program." This specificity clarifies your intentions and shows funders that you have a realistic, actionable plan.

Aligning Your Project With Funder Priorities

Once your goals are clear, aligning them with potential funders' specific interests and strategic objectives is crucial. Funders typically focus on particular areas they aim to support. By following these steps, you can align your plan with these priorities:

- **Research the funder's mission:** Learn about the funder's mission, goals, and past financed projects. All funders outline their strategic objectives directly on their websites.

- **Demonstrate alignment:** Show how your project directly supports the funder's objectives. For example, if the funder emphasizes community health, highlight how your project will improve local health outcomes by providing free weekly health screenings and wellness workshops, directly addressing the funder's goal of enhancing public health initiatives.

- **Use funders' language:** Use keywords and phrases from the funder's mission statement and guidelines in your proposal. For instance, if a funder emphasizes "community health," use this exact phrase in your proposal to show that you understand their priorities and how your project uniquely fulfills their mission goals.

- **Support your project with data and research:** Emphasize its necessity by including relevant data. For example, if you're proposing a literacy initiative for kids with ADHD, use statistics showing that approximately 25-40% of children with ADHD experience significant reading and writing difficulties, directly impacting their academic performance (Chan et al., 2023). This evidence will make your proposal more convincing and credible.

- **Outline expected outcomes:** Clearly state the outcomes you expect to achieve and how they align with and further the funder's goals. For instance, if a funder is interested in sustainable energy solutions, explain how your project involves developing solar-powered water purification systems for rural areas. Detail how this innovative solution addresses clean energy and water access. Describe the expected outcomes, such as the number of communities benefiting, reduced waterborne diseases, and decreased reliance on non-renewable energy sources.

You increase your likelihood of securing the grant with a project that adds unique value aligned with the funder's goals. This thoughtful approach shows that you've done your homework and demonstrates your commitment to making a real impact with their support. Now that your goals and objectives are in sync with funder priorities, it's time to consider the methods and activities that will bring your project to life.

Methods and Activities: How You'll Do It

When detailing your project methods and activities in a grant proposal, you're laying out the blueprint for achieving your goals. You must convince the funder that your approach is feasible, well-planned, and precise. Begin by detailing each activity, outlining the steps you'll take, the resources you'll use, and the timeline you'll follow. Funders want to see how you will deliver your promises without ambiguities.

For example, suppose you're seeking a grant to launch an after-school art program. In that case, you'll need to specify how many sessions you'll hold, what materials are required, and who will lead the sessions. A strong proposal might cite research showing that structured after-school programs can increase student engagement by up to 60%. Detailing your methods this way indicates that you've done your homework. It reassures the funder that their investment will lead to tangible results.

Ensuring feasibility is another critical aspect. Small organizations often operate with limited resources, so your plan needs to demonstrate that you can achieve your objectives within your means. Funders will look for a realistic budget and a clear explanation of how you'll manage potential challenges. If similar projects have succeeded with your proposed methods, mention this to bolster your case.

Now that you've outlined how to execute your project, the next step is tracking its progress. This leads us to the evaluation plan—how you'll measure success and show that your project has achieved its goals. Let's explore how to create a robust evaluation plan that will satisfy even the most detail-oriented funder.

Evaluation Plans: Measuring Success

It's easy to get swept up in the excitement of project planning while writing your grant proposal. However, focusing on the evaluation plan and assessing your project critically is crucial. Think of it as your roadmap to success, ensuring that all your hard work leads to tangible outcomes. A practical evaluation plan measures not just the completion of a project but also its impact. Funders want assurance that their money is making a difference, and a carefully designed evaluation plan provides that proof.

Start by developing clear, measurable objectives. If you're launching a community literacy program, don't just aim to "improve reading skills." Instead, set a target: "increase reading comprehension scores by 15% among participants within six months." That specificity guides your project and clarifies what success looks like and what you will measure.

Gather data using a mix of qualitative and quantitative techniques. Conduct surveys, interviews, and focus groups to gain insights into participants' experiences. At the same time, pre- and post-assessments offer complex numbers to back up your claims. Organizations using robust evaluation methods increase their chances of securing repeat funding, as funders value transparency and evidence of impact.

For a community literacy program, pre-assessments might include initial reading level tests, comprehension quizzes, and surveys to gauge participants' attitudes toward reading. Post-assessments could involve re-testing reading levels, follow-up comprehension quizzes, and surveys to measure changes in participants' confidence and interest in reading. By comparing the results from these assessments, you can demonstrate the program's effectiveness and the progress made by participants.

Remember, tools like online survey platforms and data analysis software are your friends here. They help you efficiently collect and analyze data despite limited resources. Be sure to include evaluation support in your budget—many funders understand that good evaluation requires investment.

For a community literacy program, examples of helpful tools include online survey platforms like SurveyMonkey (URL: surveymonkey.com) or Google Forms (URL: google.com/forms/about/) for collecting participant feedback and pre/post-assessment data. You can also use data analysis software like Excel or SPSS to track reading level improvements and analyze trends in comprehension scores. Additionally, platforms like Zoom (URL: zoom.us) or Microsoft Teams (URL: teams.microsoft.com) can be invaluable for conducting virtual focus groups or interviews, allowing you to gather qualitative insights even when in-person meetings aren't feasible.

Let's discuss the specifics of budgeting and focus on the essentials. Securing the necessary funds is crucial to moving your plans forward. Let's discuss how to build a budget that supports your project and assures funders that you can manage their money effectively.

Budgets: Show Me the Money!

The budget is where the project truly takes shape in grant writing. You've outlined a need and crafted a compelling narrative, but now it's time to show funders exactly where their money will go. Think of the budget as your project's blueprint. It reflects your understanding of the project's financial needs and demonstrates your ability to manage funds effectively.

To create a realistic and sound budget, break down every aspect of your project into manageable pieces. For example, suppose you're seeking a grant for a community literacy program. In that case, you must consider costs like staff salaries, materials, venue rental, and marketing expenses. Funders appreciate when you allocate every dollar with a clear and specific purpose, so be thorough and transparent. Successful grant applications have detailed and itemized budgets, showing that specificity pays off.

Clarity is crucial when presenting financial information. For instance, instead of listing "program expenses," break it down into "books for students," "training materials," and "instructor fees." This approach not only makes your budget clear but also helps funders visualize the impact of their investment.

Example under Instructor fees: five teachers at $25 per hour for three-hour sessions, two days a week.

Ensure that budget notes are provided for every expense. If you're requesting $5,000 for technology upgrades, describe these upgrades in detail, including the cost per item and quantity. Budgets with well-explained notes are the backbone of all successful grant proposals.

Your budget is more than just numbers; it's a powerful narrative highlighting the means to your project's success. Ensure it's as straightforward and compelling as the rest of your proposal.

Action Items

- Start by defining your project's core components—vision, mission, and goals—just like finding the corner pieces of a jigsaw puzzle.

- Clearly define the project's need by crafting a compelling statement of need to show why your project is vital and urgent.

- Set SMART objectives by making your goals specific, measurable, achievable, relevant, and time-bound to ensure clarity and feasibility.

- Incorporate relevant statistics and research to provide strong evidence of need and show why your project is vital and urgent.

- Outline expected outcomes and impacts that fulfill the funder's goals.

- Develop a detailed methods and activities plan that breaks down the steps you'll take, ensuring funders understand your approach is both feasible and well-planned.

- Create a robust evaluation plan using qualitative and quantitative methods to measure your project's success and impact.

- Build a clear, itemized budget that reflects your project's financial needs, using simple language and clear budget notes for each expense.

Now that you've meticulously crafted each grant proposal section, it's time to shift gears and focus on polishing your work. This is where you refine your language, check for consistency, and ensure that every detail aligns perfectly with the funder's expectations. Proposal crafting focuses on delivering a clear, professional, and persuasive presentation. Let's dive into the next chapter to uncover the final steps to make your proposal stand out and shine.

Chapter 7:

Polishing Your Proposal

You've completed the first draft of your grant proposal, and it feels like you've been through a tough battle. The words are there, but they're not entirely playing nice together. Your sentences are a bit like a messy desk—everything you need is somewhere in the pile, but finding it? That's another story. So, you take a deep breath, grab your red pen, and get to work. Polishing your proposal is like buffing a diamond—time-consuming, sure, but the sparkle? Worth it.

Polish Your Proposal With Effective Editing Tips

When writing a grant application, editing and proofreading can make or break the result. A well-crafted proposal communicates your ideas clearly and demonstrates your professionalism and attention to detail—qualities that grant reviewers appreciate. Here's how to ensure your proposal shines.

Practical Techniques for Editing and Proofreading

- **Take a breather before editing:** Take a break to return to your work with a fresh perspective, which helps you quickly spot oversights and inconsistencies. It's a vital step, especially after long writing sessions, to help you see your work from a first-time reader's perspective.

- **Read your proposal aloud:** Reading your text aloud compels you to slow down and focus on each word, helping you catch awkward phrases, run-on sentences, and grammatical errors that might slip past when reading silently. Using text-to-speech software, like Natural Reader (URL: naturalreaders.com/online/), to hear your proposal in a computer-generated voice can reveal issues you might otherwise overlook.

- **Concentrate on one class of mistakes at a time:** When proofreading, focus on one blunder type at a time to maintain clarity and efficiency. Begin with content. Did you answer the questions? Then, proceed with grammar and punctuation, then proceed to sentence structure, clarity, and formatting. This approach ensures that you address every question, maintain consistent headings, and verify the accuracy of your numerical data.

- **Review for clarity and consistency:** Your proposal must be crystal clear and consistent throughout. Ensure each paragraph concentrates on a central concept, and define all terms as needed. Additionally, maintain consistency in your terminology, formatting, and style throughout the document. A clear and consistent proposal helps grant reviewers quickly locate the necessary information.

- **Seek feedback:** Invite someone else to review your proposal to catch errors you might overlook and to provide insights on enhancing clarity and impact. Ask someone unfamiliar with your project to ensure they can easily understand the key points. Their feedback can significantly refine your proposal.

Common Mistakes to Watch Out For

- **Answer the questions:** Many grant seekers fail to provide clear answers because they focus on sharing every detail they believe is essential. Ensure that grant reviewers can easily find the information they need by giving them what they want to know, not just what you want to share.

- **Ignoring the instructions:** One of the most common yet easily preventable mistakes in grant writing is not adhering to the funder's guidelines. If you exceed the page limit or ignore the specified format, reviewers might reject your proposal outright. To prevent issues, strictly adhere to all policies, including specified page limits and required sections.

- **Ignoring typos and grammatical blunders:** Typos and grammatical mistakes can sabotage your proposal's professionalism and credibility. Even with solid content, such errors can leave a negative impression. While apps like spell checkers are practical, they aren't foolproof. Manual proofreading is crucial for catching mistakes that automated tools might overlook, like homophones or context-specific errors.

- **Using jargon and complex language:** While you may be familiar with the terminology in your field, grant reviewers might not be. Use precise and concise language to ensure your grant reviewer comprehends your message without feeling confused or left out. Aim for clear, straightforward language that conveys your message effectively, ensuring your proposal is easily understood and well-received.

- **Skipping the evaluation section:** Many proposals fail because they do not include a clear plan for evaluating the project's success. Funders expect a comprehensive evaluation plan in your proposal that clearly outlines how you will measure your project's impact and ensure its long-term sustainability. Make sure this plan aligns with their specific expectations.

- **Failing to review and revise:** Finally, never submit your first draft. You need to go through multiple rounds of review since editing and proofreading are iterative processes. Each pass allows you to refine your proposal further, ensuring it is as polished and compelling as possible before submission.

These suggestions will guide you in crafting a proposal that not only meets but also exceeds your reviewers' expectations. Now that your proposal is polished and error-free, let's enhance your narrative with visual aids. Next, we'll explore using visual aids to make your proposal more compelling.

Visual Aids: Using Charts, Graphs, and Images

When crafting a grant proposal, the power of visual aids—charts, graphs, and images—cannot be overstated. Online applications often have strict limitations on characters, formatting, and space for responses. When appropriate, visual aids can be referred to in your text and included as attachments. They can elevate your narrative, making complex data more digestible and your proposal more persuasive. Not all visuals are equally effective; you must incorporate them strategically to achieve a significant impact.

Insider tip: Ensure that each response to the questions is textually complete. Treat visual aids as supplementary materials unless the funder explicitly requests them.

How to Incorporate Visual Aids Effectively

First, let's talk about placement. For example, if you're discussing a budget, a pie chart that visually breaks down the funding allocation can help your grant reviewers grasp the financials quickly. You can include a pie chart as an attachment, clearly labeled as "Budget Attachment #1." Similarly, if you're outlining your project timeline, a Gantt chart can visually represent the project's phases, making it easier for the reader to understand the workflow and deadlines. You can include a Gantt chart labeled "Project Description Attachment #1."

Note: Refer to Appendix B for a sample of a budget pie chart.

Next, ensure that your visuals are simple yet informative. Overly complex graphs or cluttered images can confuse rather than clarify. According to a study by the Nielsen Norman Group, users pay more attention to images that carry information and ignore those that don't add value (Nielsen, 2010). So, opt for clear, concise visuals that convey your message at a glance.

Another crucial aspect is consistency. Your visual aids should follow a uniform style throughout the proposal, using the same color schemes, fonts, and sizes. Consistency makes your proposal look more professional and helps reinforce your brand identity, primarily if you're representing an organization.

Add captions to your visuals to provide context, helping grant reviewers quickly understand what they see and why it matters. For instance, a bar graph showing the year-over-year increase in beneficiaries should be captioned with something like "Yearly Growth in Beneficiaries, 2019-2023" to guide the grant reviewer's eye.

Examples of Impactful Visuals

Let's dive into some specific examples of visuals that can make your proposal shine.

- **Pie charts for budget breakdown:** A pie chart illustrates how your budget distributes funds across various categories. For instance, if you're requesting funding for an education initiative, your pie chart could show percentages of funds allocated to teacher salaries, student materials, technology, and administrative costs. This visual breakdown helps the reviewer quickly understand your financial plan without reading dense text.

- **Gantt charts for project timelines:** A Gantt chart effectively illustrates your project timeline. It lets you visually map out each project phase, from initial planning to execution and evaluation. For example, if your project involves community outreach, your Gantt chart might show a timeline that includes phases like "Community Surveys," "Program Development," "Pilot Testing," and "Program Rollout." This visual aid not only makes your proposal more organized but also demonstrates that you have a clear, actionable plan.

- **Infographics for data representation:** An infographic can be an excellent choice if you need to present a lot of data. Infographics use a blend of images, icons, and text to present complex information in an appealing way visually. For instance, if your grant proposal involves a health initiative, an infographic could show statistics on health outcomes, the impact of previous programs, and projected improvements with the new funding. Research shows that infographics are 30 times more likely to be read than text, making them compelling for data-heavy sections (*How Infographics*, 2017).

- **Photos and illustrations for storytelling:** A picture is worth a thousand words. Including photos or illustrations that tell the story of your work can make an emotional bond with the grant reviewer. For instance, if your grant proposal is for a performing arts program, a photo of students passionately rehearsing a dance or theater performance can effectively convey the impact of your project. Just be sure that any images, videos, or audio examples you use are high-quality and relevant to the content.

- **Work samples for individual artists:** Including work samples is crucial, especially for individual artists. These samples should showcase past work relevant to the project you're proposing. For example, if you're a composer seeking funding to write an opera, submit samples demonstrating your skills in creating similar works, such as musical theatre. Ensure your samples are high quality, clearly labeled, and properly cued up.

Remember that grant reviewers read stacks of proposals. Making your proposal memorable and engaging is always a win. Visual aids, when used correctly, are a powerful tool in your grant writing arsenal.

Now that you've learned the art of visual aids, it's time to bring in fresh perspectives. Having more people review your proposal will make it stronger. Let's explore how getting feedback can elevate your grant writing to the next level.

Getting Feedback: The More Eyes, the Better

In grant writing, getting feedback isn't just helpful—it's essential. When you've spent hours crafting your proposal, it's easy to miss minor errors or overlook areas that need clarification. Feedback is crucial in elevating your proposal from good to excellent by incorporating insights from various perspectives.

Strategies for Soliciting and Incorporating Feedback

The first step in effectively leveraging feedback is knowing how to ask for it. Start by identifying the right people to review your proposal. These should be individuals who understand the context of your grant application and have experience in grant writing or the specific field your project addresses. You can ask colleagues, mentors, or members of your organization's board of directors to review your proposal. The key is to find those who can provide constructive, detailed feedback.

Once you've identified your reviewers, be specific about what you need. Instead of asking for general feedback, direct your reviewers to focus on particular sections or aspects of the proposal. For example, ask one person to look at the clarity of your objectives. Another reviewer might concentrate on evaluating the feasibility of your budget. This targeted approach ensures that you get comprehensive feedback without overwhelming any single reviewer.

Incorporating feedback can be problematic, particularly when it contradicts your original concept. However, it's crucial to remain open-minded. Critically assess the feedback—address issues that multiple reviewers consistently identify. You'll sometimes need to make tough decisions about what to keep and revise, but remember that your goal is strengthening the proposal.

The Power of Many Eyes

Getting more people to review your proposal increases your chances of success. Each person will have a different lens when reviewing your proposal. Ask one person to focus on the technical details. Another person can review your proposal to ensure it aligns well with the funder's goals. Combining these perspectives allows you to create a technically sound proposal strategically aligned with the grant's goals.

The impact of multiple perspectives in the grant writing process is significant, so make sure to leverage this feedback effectively. By soliciting and incorporating feedback and using peer review methods effectively, you can significantly improve your proposal's quality and increase your chances of securing funding. After all, when it comes to grant writing, the more eyes, the better.

Action Items

- Read your grant proposal aloud to catch awkward phrases and grammatical errors.

- Include relevant work samples to showcase your experience and capabilities.

- Clearly label all attachments to ensure easy navigation for reviewers.

- Keep your proposal's terminology, formatting, and style consistent from start to finish.

- Listen to your proposal using a text-to-speech tool to help you catch issues easily overlooked when reading silently.

- Solicit feedback from individuals experienced in grant writing or your specific field.

- Create a feedback log to track comments and your responses.

- Conduct multiple rounds of proofreading and revision before submission.

With your proposal now polished, focus on the final stage: submission. This chapter will walk you through the essential steps to ensure your grant proposal is submitted correctly, meets all criteria, and boosts your chances of getting to "yes."

Chapter 8:

Submission Success

You've finally hit that "submit" button, feeling relief and triumph—until you realize you've attached the wrong file. Panic sets in as you imagine your proposal landing in a grant review session with incorrect information. You scramble to fix it, but you discover there is no undo button in grant submissions. Lesson learned: double-check everything before sending it out into the world!

But don't worry—mastering digital submissions is easier than it sounds. Next, we'll guide you through navigating online portals like a pro, ensuring your proposal lands precisely where it should.

Digital Submissions: Navigating Online Portals

Navigating the world of digital submissions can feel like stepping into a maze. With the proper techniques, you can send your grant proposal without issues. Here's how to make your digital submissions seamless and stress-free.

Tips for Successful Digital Submissions

Always begin by carefully checking the submission procedures. Each grantmaker has specific requirements, and overlooking even a minor detail can disqualify your application. Pay close attention to file formats, naming conventions, and any required attachments. For instance, some portals may require PDFs, while others might prefer Word documents if they ask for a specific file name format—like "OrganizationName_GrantProposal2024"—follow it to the letter. You need to focus on these seemingly minor details to ensure your proposal gets reviewed.

Before you hit "submit," do a final check of your uploaded documents. Ensure your proposal is thorough, free of typos, and properly formatted. This simple step can save you from submitting a less-than-perfect application.

A key element is managing your time proactively so you aren't rushing to submit your proposal at the last minute. Online portals can experience technical issues when many people try to upload files simultaneously. By submitting early, you demonstrate professionalism and preparedness and avoid these potential issues.

Always check for a confirmation message or email after you hit the "submit" button. This confirmation confirms receipt of your proposal and reassures you that your submission was successful. If you don't receive a reply, follow up with the grantmaker to verify your submission. This proactive step ensures you won't miss an opportunity due to a technical issue.

Common Issues and How to Avoid Them

One common issue with digital submissions is file size limitations. Many portals have strict file size limits and will reject your documents if they exceed them. To avoid this problem, compress your files before submission. You can use tools like Adobe Acrobat or free online services to reduce file sizes while maintaining quality (URL: get.adobe.com/reader/).

Another issue is browser compatibility. Some online portals work best with specific browsers. If you're having trouble, try using a different browser or updating your current one. Always check the portal's recommended browser settings to avoid any last-minute surprises.

Technical glitches, like server timeouts or slow uploads, are also common. These issues often occur during peak times, especially when submission deadlines are approaching. Submit your proposal early to avoid being caught in a digital traffic jam near the deadline.

By following these tips and being aware of common issues, you can confidently navigate digital submission portals and ensure that your grant proposal reaches its destination without any setbacks.

Now that you've mastered the digital side of grant submissions, let's not forget about the old-school method. Next, we'll explore when paper submissions are still the way to go and how to ensure your hard copy proposal makes just as strong an impression.

Paper Submissions: When Old School Still Rules

In a digital age where online submissions dominate, paper submissions might seem like a relic of the past. However, for many grant funders, especially those who appreciate tradition, paper submissions still hold their ground. If you're working with a funder who prefers old-school methods, nailing your paper submission can set you apart. Here's how to ensure your submission meets and exceeds expectations.

Best Practices for Paper Submissions

First and foremost, start by understanding the funder's detailed instructions. Foundations and government agencies set guidelines, specifying everything from the type of paper to the binding style. Some prefer simple staples, while others require a more professional presentation, such as spiral binding or a folder. By following these guidelines meticulously, you demonstrate your attention to detail and increase your chances of making a good impression.

Next, consider the quality of your materials. This is where the tactile experience of a paper submission can work in your favor. Invest in high-quality, heavyweight paper—typically 24-pound or 28-pound stock. The texture and weight can subconsciously communicate professionalism and attention to detail. Choosing the suitable ink is crucial. Use a high-resolution printer to ensure crisp and clear text. Avoid colors—stick to black ink unless the guidelines specify otherwise.

Formatting also plays a crucial role. A well-organized and neat document is uncomplicated and leaves a lasting impression. Use a standard font like Times New Roman or Arial, set at 12-point size, with 1-inch margins on all sides. Double-spacing is usually preferred, but always adhere to the specific instructions provided by the funder.

Number your pages, and include your organization's name or project title in a header or footer for easy reference.

Ensure you include all required documents in the specified order. Use dividers or tabs to separate sections, making navigating your submission easy for the reviewer. If you're submitting multiple copies, ensure each is identical and pristine. Even a tiny error or inconsistency can be a red flag to a meticulous grant reviewer.

Finally, timing is everything. Unlike digital submissions, where you can hit send at the last minute, paper submissions require extra time for preparation and mailing. Non-compliance with submission guidelines, including missed deadlines, leads to the rejection of grant applications. To avoid this pitfall, send your submission well before the deadline. Choose a reliable courier service with tracking to ensure timely and secure delivery of your documents.

Ensuring Your Submission Stands Out

Standing out in a sea of paper submissions requires a blend of creativity and adherence to guidelines. One effective way to differentiate your submission is through a compelling cover letter. This letter briefly introduces your project, highlights its significance, and mentions any standout elements of your proposal. You have one opportunity to grab the reviewer's attention before they start examining the details.

Additionally, consider including an executive summary at the beginning of your proposal. This one-page summary should provide a high-level overview of your project, including its goals, methodology, and expected outcomes. Reviewers often appreciate a well-crafted summary that gives them a quick grasp of your project's value.

Include visual aids where they add value. A relevant chart, graph, or image can make complex information easier to understand and break up the text. Ensure that all visuals directly support your key points. Overloading your submission with unnecessary graphics can have the opposite effect, making it look cluttered and unfocused.

Proofreading is crucial, whether your proposal is online or on paper. Spelling, grammar, or formatting errors can reduce the professionalism of your proposal. Review your work thoroughly multiple times before submitting it, and, if possible, have somebody else proofread it. Another person can offer a fresh perspective and catch mistakes you might have overlooked.

Now that you've learned the art of paper submissions, it's time to think about what comes next. After all, submitting your proposal is only the beginning. Following up is essential to staying on the funder's radar and boosting your chances of success. Next, we'll explore the dos and don'ts of follow-up etiquette and how to maintain a positive and professional relationship with potential funders.

Follow-Up Etiquette: Staying on the Funder's Radar

After you've submitted your grant proposal, the waiting game begins. But sitting idly by isn't your best strategy. Following up with funders can make a significant difference in ensuring your proposal gets the attention it deserves. Here's how to do it professionally, keeping you on the funder's radar without overstepping.

Building Ongoing Relationships With Funders

To build ongoing relationships, keep funders updated on your project's progress. If you secure funding, regularly update the funders on your milestones and demonstrate the impact their support is creating. Even if your proposal isn't selected, sharing how your project progressed can open the door for future opportunities.

Engage with funders outside the grant cycle as well. Attend events they host, interact with them on social media, and participate in their webinars or workshops. These interactions demonstrate your commitment to the relationship beyond financial support.

Following up and building relationships with funders are critical to successful grant writing. By following up professionally and nurturing ongoing connections, you position yourself as a proactive and reliable partner, increasing your chances of securing funding not just once but repeatedly.

Action Items

- Review submission guidelines thoroughly to ensure compliance with all requirements.

- Double-check all documents for completeness, accuracy, and formatting before uploading.

- Submit your proposal early to avoid last-minute technical issues or server overload.

- Use a recommended browser for the online portal to avoid compatibility issues.

- Confirm that you've received a submission confirmation email or message.

Now that you've successfully submitted your proposal and followed up like a pro, the hard part begins: waiting. The period between submission and decision can be nerve-wracking. Still, it's also an opportunity to prepare for what comes next. Let's explore how to navigate this waiting game with patience and strategy.

Chapter 9:

The Waiting Game

You hit "submit" on your grant proposal, and the waiting game begins. It's like watching a pot of water boil, except this pot holds your hopes and dreams and that perfect program you've spent countless hours crafting. As the days pass, you obsessively check your email, hoping for that golden "Congratulations!" to pop up. But instead, your inbox is just a barren wasteland of newsletters and spam. Why not do something productive rather than stare at your screen all day?

What to Do While You Wait: Taking Control of the Waiting Period

You've submitted your grant proposal, and now you're in that nerve-wracking waiting period where time seems to stretch endlessly. However, this is not the time to sit idly by; it's an opportunity to keep busy productively and set yourself up for success, no matter the outcome. Here's how you can make the most of this time.

Productive Activities During the Waiting Period

Instead of obsessively refreshing your inbox, focus your energy on tasks that will benefit you and your organization, regardless of the grant's outcome. One productive way to spend this time is planning your next grant proposal. Researching new funding opportunities and drafting initial ideas will not only keep you busy but also keep you ahead of the curve. You can explore databases like Grants.gov (URL: grants.gov) or Foundation Directory Online (URL: fconline.foundationcenter.org) to identify potential funders whose interests align with your projects. Moreover, starting early allows you to craft a more compelling narrative backed by thorough research and a clear understanding of the potential funder's priorities. Organizations that regularly pursue new grant opportunities are more successful in securing funding.

Networking is another critical activity during the waiting period. Strengthen your relationships with existing partners and actively work on building new ones during this time. Attend relevant conferences, webinars, or local networking events where you can meet potential collaborators or funders. Building a solid network can provide invaluable insights, potential partnerships, and direct funding opportunities.

You should carefully review your internal processes. This could involve reassessing your project management strategies, evaluating your team's performance, or revisiting your organization's mission and vision to ensure they align with your current objectives.

Finally, consider using this time to invest in professional development. Whether you attend a workshop on grant writing, take an online course on nonprofit management, or read up on the latest trends in your field, expanding your knowledge and skills will make you a more effective leader and grant writer. Coursera (URL: coursera.org) and Nonprofit Ready (URL: nonprofitready.org) offer a variety of free or low-cost courses that can help you sharpen your skills.

Preparing for Possible Outcomes

As you keep busy, it's also wise to prepare for the possible outcomes of your grant application. This preparation ensures that you are ready to take immediate action as soon as you hear back from the funder.

You'll need to hit the ground running if your grant is approved. Use this time to fine-tune your project plan, fire up your team, and start laying the groundwork for the project's implementation. Create a detailed timeline, assign specific roles, and ensure all necessary resources are available. This proactive approach will allow you to move quickly and efficiently when the funds are released.

Prepare yourself for the possibility that your proposal might not secure funding. Although this outcome can be disappointing, it's not the journey's end. Start by considering alternative funding sources—perhaps through crowdfunding, local businesses, or even revising and resubmitting your proposal to another funder. Use rejection as a chance to learn by requesting feedback from the funder. This will help you identify areas where your proposal fell short, allowing you to apply those insights to strengthen future submissions.

Insider tip: Requesting panel comments shows the funder that you're genuinely interested in learning and improving from this experience. Some funders also seek volunteers to serve as panelists. Volunteering for this role is an excellent way to gain insights into what makes a successful grant application by seeing the process from the funder's perspective.

Being proactive and staying engaged during the waiting period helps pass the time and positions you and your organization for success, regardless of the outcome.

Now that you're making the most of your waiting period, it's time to consider the pro move—welcoming new and potential funders to see your work in action. Prepare to impress them with a well-organized, informative visit.

Site Visits: Showcasing Your Organization's Importance

You roll out the red carpet for you and your organization when you host a site visit for potential funders. It's your chance to shine, to showcase your work, and to build a relationship that could lead to long-term support. But how do you ensure your site visit leaves a lasting, positive impression? Let's break it down.

Tips for Hosting Site Visits

- **Prepare your team (or yourself):** Every detail counts if you're an individual or part of a small team. Before the visit, thoroughly prepare yourself or your small team. If it's just you, ensure you're well-versed in every aspect of your program, from its goals to its technical details. If you have a small team, assign specific roles—perhaps one person can handle the technical questions. At the same time, another focuses on leading the tour. This practice ensures you show a cohesive and well-organized image, regardless of your operation's size.

- **Plan a route:** You might have limited facilities as a small organization or individual grant seeker, but that can work to your advantage. Choose the locations that best showcase the impact of your work, whether it's a small community space, your office, or the direct area where your program operates. Keep the route short but impactful, ensuring each stop highlights a unique aspect of your program. If possible, arrange a brief interaction with beneficiaries or demonstrate your services live. Adding a personal touch can create a lasting impression.

- **Have materials ready:** Given that your resources might be limited, focus on creating concise and powerful materials. A one-page summary, fact sheet, or small brochure can go a long way. Use infographics or short videos to help your message stick, as these convey complex information quickly and memorably. Even if your budget is small, these visual tools can significantly convey the impact of your work.

- **Practice your pitch:** As an individual or small organization, you may have limited opportunities to make your case, so perfecting your pitch is crucial. Rehearse how you'll articulate the value and impact of your program. Keep your message clear, concise, and compelling—funders are likely visiting multiple sites, so making your pitch memorable is vital. If you're working alone, consider practicing with a friend or mentor to iron out any issues. If you have a small team, do a complete run-through together.

- **Be hospitable:** Hospitality doesn't have to be elaborate to be effective. Provide refreshments and create a comfortable, conversation-friendly environment. Even if you're operating on a tight budget, thoughtful gestures like these can leave a strong, positive impression. Your attention to detail demonstrates the care and professionalism you put into your work.

- **Follow up promptly:** After the visit, make it a priority to send a follow-up email promptly. Convey your appreciation for their time and briefly summarize the critical points discussed. If the funders requested additional information, include it in your follow-up. Quick and thoughtful follow-up is crucial for individuals and small organizations—it shows your commitment. It keeps your organization fresh in the funders' minds.

Making a Positive Impression on Funders

First impressions are important, particularly when negotiating with potential funders. They form opinions about your organization as soon as they arrive at your site. Here's how you can ensure those opinions are positive:

- **Show impact, not just process:** Funders are interested in outcomes. While it's essential to demonstrate how your program operates, focus on its impact. Introduce someone who has experienced a positive change in their life because of your work rather than just showing your facility. Real stories of impact resonate more deeply on an emotional level than statistics alone.

- **Be transparent:** Funders appreciate honesty. If your organization faces challenges, don't avoid discussing them. However, frame these challenges in a way that highlights your proactive approach to finding solutions. Transparency builds trust and shows that you are not just presenting a polished facade but are ready to tackle real issues head-on.

Insider tip: When you share the full scope of your project—its successes, challenges, and even the flaws—you provide funders with a clear view into your world, offering them an opportunity to see how they can contribute. Even if they can't support your project directly, they might be able to connect you with another funder who can, which can be an invaluable introduction. Keep in mind that people fund people, and funders are people too.

- **Engage in dialogue:** Site visits shouldn't be one-sided tours. Encourage funders to ask questions and provide their insights. Engage directly with them to address their concerns and make them feel appreciated.

- **Express gratitude:** It might sound simple, but thanking funders for their time and interest is crucial. Tell them you value their potential support and that their visit greatly benefits your organization. Genuine gratitude can set a positive tone for future interactions.

Now that you've mastered hosting a successful site visit, it's time to face another reality of the grant writing process: rejections. How do you handle rejection?

Handling Rejections: Bouncing Back Stronger

Rejection is a common experience in grant writing, but it doesn't have to hold you back. Your response to setbacks can shape your future success. Embrace rejection with resilience and a growth mindset to transform challenges into opportunities for learning and improvement.

Dealing With Rejection Positively

Rejection stings. When your grant proposal gets turned down, it's easy to feel disheartened, significantly when you've invested time, energy, and passion into your project. However, rejection can become a stepping stone to success if you handle it positively instead of letting it be a roadblock.

Rejection doesn't determine your worth or reduce the significance of your project. Funders often receive many more proposals than they can support, and the decision may come down to factors beyond your control. Embrace this reality, and rather than dwelling on the rejection, focus on what you can control—your response.

Insider tip: Think of a rejection as a "not yet" instead of a "no." Many funders don't grant first-time applicants but prefer to get to know you and your work over time. Additionally, funders often have internal cycles influenced by factors like geographic location, demographics, project types, and previous funding decisions—details that may not be apparent to applicants.

A positive approach to rejection involves viewing it as a learning experience. Research from the University of Pennsylvania shows that people with a growth mindset are likelier to persevere and achieve lasting success after setbacks (Berg et al., 2022). They see rejection as an opportunity to learn and enhance their skills rather than as a failure.

Take a moment to acknowledge your feelings—frustration, disappointment, or even anger. Feeling this way is natural, but don't let these emotions dominate. Focus on taking productive action by reminding yourself why you began this journey. Revisit your organization's mission and the impact you aim to achieve. This approach can reignite your motivation and help you focus on the bigger picture.

Engage in self-care activities to help manage the emotional impact of rejection. Take a walk, talk to a supportive friend, or dive into a hobby you love. These actions can offer a vital mental reset, enabling you to approach the situation more clearly and positively.

Learning From Feedback and Improving Future Proposals

Now that you've processed the rejection, it's time to turn it into a valuable learning experience. If the funder provided feedback, use it as a blueprint for improvement. This feedback is gold—it's insight directly from the people who review your proposals and can guide you in making your next submission even stronger.

Start by carefully analyzing the feedback. Did the reviewers mention any specific areas where your proposal fell short? Your budget might not have been clear, your objectives may have differed from the funder's priorities, or your narrative might have needed a stronger, more compelling story. This moment offers you the opportunity to learn and adjust your approach.

You can enhance your proposals by studying successful ones for comparison. Many organizations share their winning projects online. Study these examples to identify what the funder cares about and how these projects resonate with those values. You might notice trends in the project descriptions like clear and concise language, strong evidence of overlooked needs, or innovative approaches that align with the funder's mission. You can significantly improve your chances of success by integrating these elements into your future proposals.

In addition to direct feedback, consider reflecting on the broader context of your proposal within the field or community you're working in. This process involves understanding trends, shifts in funding priorities, and emerging needs within your sector. By staying informed about these larger dynamics, you can tailor your future proposals to be more relevant and timely. Engaging with professional networks or attending industry conferences can provide valuable insights into these trends, helping you align your proposals with current priorities and increasing your chances of success.

Finally, consider the possibility of pivoting your approach. Suppose the funder rejected your proposal due to a lack of alignment with their priorities. You should reassess your approach and consider rethinking your strategy. Look for other funding opportunities that better match your project's goals. Expanding your funding sources can boost your chances of success. Individuals and organizations that apply to multiple funders rather than relying on a single source are more resilient and better positioned to identify the best funders and secure the necessary resources.

Remember, the road to securing funding is rarely a straight path. Rejections are part of the journey but don't define your goal. By handling rejection positively and learning from the experience, you can bounce back stronger and more prepared for the next opportunity. Keep refining your approach, stay resilient, and continue to pursue your organization's mission with passion and determination. Your next proposal might be the one that opens the door to the support you need.

Action Items

- Start planning your next grant proposal by researching new funding opportunities and drafting initial ideas.

- Strengthen your relationships with current partners and connect with potential collaborators or funders.

- Attend workshops, take online courses, or stay updated on industry trends to invest in your professional development.

- Review your organization's internal processes thoroughly to identify opportunities for improvement.

- If your proposal doesn't secure funding, explore alternative financial support options, such as crowdfunding or partnering with local businesses.

- Request feedback from funders on rejected proposals and use their insights to improve your future submissions.

- To diversify your funding sources and increase resilience, explore other funding opportunities that better align with your project's goals.

Winning a grant is a testament to your hard work and dedication, reflecting the effort you've put into your endeavors. But the real work begins after the celebration. Now, focus on executing your project successfully, using every dollar efficiently, and maximizing your impact.

Chapter 10:

When You Win

Winning a grant is more than a milestone; it reflects your effort and commitment. It's like finding a golden ticket in your inbox, a moment that should fill you with pride and a sense of accomplishment. You can almost feel the high-fives from your team and hear the imaginary applause. This is your moment, and it's more than just a quiet nod. But an essential next step is getting the word out before you celebrate. You've got the green light. Now, it's time to shine a spotlight on your success.

Celebrating Success: Sharing the Good News

Winning a grant is a momentous occasion, and effectively sharing that success can amplify your impact and solidify relationships with your stakeholders. By announcing and celebrating your grant win, you share good news, empower your supporters, and make them feel they are an important part of your journey. This ensures everyone who supports your work feels acknowledged and appreciated.

Announcing Your Grant Win

First things first: make your announcement timely and strategic. Start by notifying your internal team, ensuring everyone is on the same page before the news goes public. A coordinated internal communication plan helps prevent misinformation and sets the stage for a unified external message.

Tailor your message for different platforms and audiences when making public announcements. For instance, on social media, you can share a post with a compelling image or video, a brief description of the grant win, and a call to action for your followers to celebrate with you. Consider sending a press release, revamping your website, and sharing the news in your organization's newsletter. For a more personal touch, reach out directly to key stakeholders, including funders, partners, and community leaders, to inform them of your achievement. This approach not only shares the good news but also strengthens your relationships.

A nonprofit organization might announce its grant win by sharing a compelling story on social media, showcasing the project that will receive funding and the expected positive impact on the community. This would inform the public and create an opportunity for the organization to connect with new supporters who are passionate about the cause.

Engaging Stakeholders and Supporters

Your grant win is not just your success—it's a collective victory for everyone involved. Acknowledging your stakeholders during the celebration is a powerful way to express appreciation and strengthen trust. It's a way of saying, "You are valued and respected," to those who have supported you. Publicly acknowledge their contributions with personalized thank-you notes, social media shout-outs, or mentions in your press release.

Whether virtual or in-person, hosting an event is a fantastic way to celebrate. Invite your stakeholders, including funders, community members, and partners, to join the celebration. Use this opportunity to share your vision for the grant-funded project, discuss the next steps, and express gratitude for their support. For instance, you can share a presentation or a video that outlines the project's goals, the impact you aim to achieve, and how their support is crucial for its success. This approach engages your stakeholders and shows your commitment to transparency and communication.

Additionally, consider involving your stakeholders in the implementation process. Regular updates on the progress of the grant-funded project through newsletters or dedicated social media posts can keep your supporters engaged and informed. This open communication builds trust and can deepen their dedication to the project's success.

Now that you've shared your success and engaged your stakeholders, it's time to turn your attention to managing your grant funds effectively. Proper financial management ensures your project stays on track and meets your funder's requirements. Let's explore the best practices for managing grant funds to keep your project running smoothly and satisfy your stakeholders.

Managing Grant Funds: Best Practices

Effectively managing grant funds is crucial for individuals and small organizations. It's about making sure you use every grant dollar appropriately. Whether you're a one-person operation or a small team, how you handle grant money can make or break your credibility and future funding opportunities.

Effective Grant Fund Management

To start, set up a dedicated account for your grant funds. Keeping grant money separate from other funds makes tracking expenses more manageable. It avoids the temptation to dip into those funds for unrelated costs. For example, if you're a freelance writer awarded a grant to develop a community literacy program, put that money in a separate account to ensure every dollar goes toward that goal.

Budgeting is another critical element. Before you spend a dime, create a detailed budget that aligns with your grant proposal. The budget should account for all potential expenses, including supplies, staffing, and operational costs. Tools like Excel or Google Sheets are great for this purpose, offering simple ways to monitor and adjust your budget as needed. For small organizations, keeping a tight budget can prevent overspending and ensure that funds are available when unexpected costs arise.

Regular expense monitoring is essential. Weekly or monthly budget check-ins help catch discrepancies early on, such as higher-than-expected spending on outreach materials.

Ensuring Compliance and Accountability

Compliance with grant requirements is not optional—it's mandatory. Each grant specifies conditions for fund usage and required reporting. Make sure you understand these conditions from the start. For individuals and small organizations, non-compliance can lead to the loss of funding and damage your reputation.

To ensure compliance, document everything. Keep receipts, invoices, and any correspondence related to the grant. This documentation is crucial not only for staying organized but also for preparing the required reports. For instance, if you're running a small environmental initiative funded by a grant, you should document every expense related to materials, equipment, and volunteer stipends.

Transparency fuels accountability. Share your progress with stakeholders, whether that's through regular reports, newsletters, or social media updates. This approach ensures accountability and shows funders you're using their money as intended. Organizations that regularly communicate their progress to funders are more likely to receive repeat funding.

Finally, prepare for audits. While audits might seem daunting, they are a standard part of grant management, especially for larger grants. Audits might be less frequent for smaller organizations or individual grant seekers, but they can still happen. Being prepared with organized records and clear documentation can make the process smoother.

Reporting and Compliance: Keeping Funders Happy

Keeping your funders happy is crucial for securing future grants and building long-lasting relationships. Two critical components to achieving this outcome are developing comprehensive reports and maintaining good relationships with your funders. These tasks might seem daunting to an individual or small organization grant seeker. Still, with the right approach, you can excel and stand out.

Developing Comprehensive Reports

Your first step in keeping funders satisfied is to create detailed and accurate reports. Funders expect to see the impact of their financial support, and it's your responsibility to demonstrate it. Start by understanding the reporting requirements laid out in your grant agreement. This might include specific metrics, timelines, or financial breakdowns. You can produce reports that meet or exceed funder expectations by staying on top of these requirements.

For example, if running a community-based program, include quantitative data such as the number of participants served, outcomes achieved, and funds utilized. If your program concentrates on education, you could highlight test scores, graduation rates, or attendance improvements. Pair these numbers with qualitative data—stories or testimonials from beneficiaries that bring your program's impact to life. Funders respond positively to reports that combine data with compelling narratives, as they provide a more holistic view of the program's success.

Start compiling your report early to avoid last-minute stress. Set up a system to track your progress throughout the grant period. Regularly update your metrics and document significant milestones. This proactive approach streamlines the reporting process and helps you gather all the necessary details.

Maintaining Good Relationships With Funders

Maintaining a solid relationship with your funders goes beyond just sending in your reports. It's about communication, transparency, and showing that you value their partnership. Even outside formal reporting periods, regular updates can go a long way. A quick email or phone call to share a recent success or challenge keeps your funders in the loop and demonstrates your commitment to the project.

Transparency is key. If you encounter any issues or delays, don't shy away from sharing these with your funders. Being upfront about challenges shows that you're honest and capable of managing difficulties. Funders appreciate this transparency, allowing them to adjust expectations and offer support. They value honesty and are likelier to continue funding organizations that communicate openly about successes and setbacks.

Building personal connections with your funders can also be beneficial. Whenever possible, invite them to visit your program or attend an event. Seeing your work firsthand can strengthen their investment in your success. If in-person meetings aren't possible, consider sharing videos or virtual tours. Personal touches can significantly influence how funders view your work, especially in small organizations.

Always express your gratitude. A simple thank you goes a long way. After receiving a grant, send a personalized thank you note. At the end of the project, thank your funders again for their support and share the impact their funding made. These gestures help reinforce the positive relationship and can set the stage for future funding opportunities.

Action Items

- Ensure coordinated communication and notify your internal team about the grant win before making public announcements.

- Tailor your public announcement of the grant win to different platforms, such as social media, press releases, and newsletters, for maximum impact.

- To keep your stakeholders engaged, regularly update them through newsletters or social media posts on the progress of the grant-funded project.

- Conduct regular financial reviews to identify discrepancies and adjust spending to maintain financial accuracy and trust with funders.

- Ensure compliance with grant regulations by understanding specific requirements and setting up clear policies and procedures for documentation and reporting.

- To build trust and collaborative problem-solving, engage in proactive and transparent communication with funders, especially when challenges arise.

With your grant successfully managed and relationships with funders solidified, it's time to think beyond the grant. In the next chapter, we'll explore how to leverage your accomplishments to secure future funding, expand your impact, and ensure the sustainability of your projects.

Chapter 11:
Beyond the Grant

You've secured the grant, and the celebration is on! But now, as the confetti settles, reality sets in. You realize that winning the grant was just the beginning. Like a victorious marathon runner who suddenly remembers there's another race tomorrow, you know that managing this success is just as crucial as achieving it. The work ahead isn't just about maintaining momentum; it's about thinking beyond the dollars and planning for a future where your project thrives with the continued support of your fans and donors. That's where sustainability comes in—planning for life after the grant. Let's dive into how you can ensure your project flourishes long after the initial funding dries up.

Sustainability: Planning for Life After the Grant

Securing a grant is exhilarating, but the real challenge begins once the funds start flowing. Ensuring your project's long-term success requires a proactive approach to sustainability. You need to develop a strong plan for when the grant period concludes. Whether you're in the performing arts or launching a small business, the strategies you employ now will determine whether your project thrives or fizzles out post-grant.

Strategies for Sustaining Your Project Post-Grant

When planning a grant-funded project, it's crucial to consider sustainability long before the grant expires. From the outset, you should integrate sustainability goals into your project objectives, ensuring your initiatives can continue thriving after the grant funding is exhausted. This proactive approach, established during your project planning phase, not only sets the foundation for maintaining operations in the long term but also brings a sense of optimism and motivation as you see the potential benefits of your efforts.

It's crucial to start sustainability planning from day one. By envisioning how you will support your project post-grant, you foster a forward-thinking mindset that can significantly enhance the longevity of your efforts. This emphasis on forward-thinking can inspire you to look beyond the grant period and plan for the future, making your efforts more impactful and long-lasting.

Small businesses can also benefit from sustainability planning. Consider a local startup that receives a grant to develop a new product line. Instead of relying solely on grant funds, the startup can focus on building a loyal customer base through effective marketing strategies from the outset. By developing a subscription model, they create a continuous cash flow that sustains the business even after the grant ends. This approach allows the company to transition smoothly, avoiding the common pitfall of scrambling for funds once the initial grant period concludes and providing security and stability.

Ultimately, integrating sustainability into your project objectives is not just about securing the future of your initiatives. It's about positioning your project for continuous development and success. By planning for the long term and adopting strategies that generate ongoing revenue, you ensure that your project remains viable and impactful well beyond the life of the grant.

Diversifying Funding Sources

Relying on just one grant or funding source for your project is like walking a tightrope without a safety net—one wrong step could bring everything crashing down. Diversifying your funding isn't just recommended; it's crucial for ensuring your project's long-term sustainability. Securing financial support from multiple sources reduces the risk of losing all your funding. It protects your project from unanticipated financial lapses.

Begin by pinpointing grant prospects that align with your project's objectives. Many grants support similar initiatives, particularly in the arts and small business sectors. For instance, a nonprofit theater group that initially secured funding from a local arts council can seek additional financial backing from national foundations, corporate sponsors, or crowdfunding campaigns. This diverse funding approach ensures continued operations and opens new avenues for resources and growth opportunities.

For small businesses, diversification can mean pursuing venture capital, seeking out angel investors, or forming strategic partnerships with other organizations. Take, for instance, a small company that receives a grant to launch a new product. Once the product demonstrates success and potential for growth, the business could secure additional funding through a business loan or attracting investors. This layered approach provides a solid foundation, making the company attractive to potential backers.

Many nonprofit organizations often create endowments or reserve funds as financial cushions. These funds act as a safety net during lean periods, ensuring operations can continue even when external funding is scarce. By building a robust economic base with multiple funding sources, organizations are better equipped to weather financial storms and maintain resilience, ensuring the continued success of their projects. Diversification is the key to long-term stability and growth.

Now that you have planned to sustain your project post-grant, let's build lasting relationships with your funders. But we should clarify that building solid and lasting relationships with your funders should be a priority from the beginning of your project. These relationships are crucial for future support and continued success. Let's explore how to foster long-term connections that will keep your project thriving for years.

Building Long-Term Relationships With Funders

Forging long-term relationships with funders is necessary for securing ongoing support and ensuring your project's continued success. As in any relationship, consistency, communication, and mutual respect are vital in turning funders from one-time supporters into long-term partners. This approach builds a network of allies who share your mission and want to see you succeed, creating a sense of community and support.

Tips for Long-Term Engagement With Funders

Start by seeing your funders as partners rather than just financial backers. This mindset shift is essential. Engage with them regularly, not just when submitting a proposal or a report. Regularly update them on your project's progress, challenges, and critical milestones. For example, if you're a small theater group that received a grant to produce a play, invite your funders to rehearsals or show them behind-the-scenes footage. This makes them feel involved and shows that you value their support beyond just the financial aspect.

Another tip is to personalize your communication. Understand your funders' priorities, and craft your updates to show how your work consistently aligns with their goals. For instance, if a funder is interested in promoting women entrepreneurs, and your business received funding for a women-led initiative, keep them informed about how your project empowers women and contributes to gender equality. Funders are more likely to continue their support when they see their values upheld and advanced through the projects they fund.

It's also essential to express gratitude often and genuinely. A sincere thank you can have a powerful effect. After completing each milestone, take the time to send a personalized thank you note highlighting their support's specific implications. This shows respect for their contribution and builds a sense of shared achievement, making them feel appreciated and respected.

Turning Funders Into Long-Term Partners

Turning funders into long-term partners involves deepening the relationship over time. One effective strategy is to include funders in your organization's strategic planning. This doesn't mean they take over; you seek their advice and insights on growing and sustaining your project. For instance, a small business that received a grant for an eco-friendly initiative might invite funders to provide input on expanding the business model to include more sustainable practices. This approach values their expertise and gives them a sense of ownership in your project's success.

Another powerful approach is to demonstrate the long-term impact of their support. Use data and stories to show how their funding has made a difference in the short term and the broader community. For example, a report by the National Endowment for the Arts highlighted how grants to women-led theater companies resulted in increased representation of women in the performing arts, a long-term societal impact that funders are proud to support.

Moreover, consider ways to give back to your funders. You could offer funders exclusive event access, branding opportunities, or even the chance to name specific programs. For instance, a small nonprofit that received funding to start a community garden could name a section of the garden after a significant funder, offering them lasting recognition and a tangible connection to the project.

Building long-term relationships with funders isn't just about securing money; it's about creating a network of support that can help your project thrive for years to come. As you nurture these relationships, focusing on continuous improvement is crucial. Every grant cycle provides lessons that can refine your approach and boost your chances of success. Let's examine how to learn from each experience to keep your project progressing.

Continuous Improvement: Learning From Each Experience

Every grant cycle offers you a treasure trove of insights, whether you succeed or not. Reflecting on and learning from each experience is essential to your growth as a grant writer and as a leader of your project or organization. The key to continuous improvement lies in analyzing what worked and what didn't and how you can refine your approach for the future. Let's explore how you can turn each grant cycle into a learning opportunity that propels you toward tremendous success.

Reflecting On and Learning From Each Grant Cycle

Reflect on the entire process once you've completed your grant application. Start by asking yourself some critical questions: Did your proposal align perfectly with the funder's priorities? Did you clearly articulate your goals and outcomes? Did you follow all submission guidelines and meet the deadlines? Evaluating these aspects can help you pinpoint your strengths and identify areas for improvement.

For example, consider the case of Marsha, a small business owner who applied for an arts grant to support her budding theater company. After her first unsuccessful attempt, Marsha took a step back to evaluate her proposal. She realized that while her artistic vision was clear, she had overlooked some critical details in her budget and timeline, which made her application less compelling. By reflecting on these gaps, Marsha was able to refine her proposal in her next attempt, which ultimately led to securing the grant.

Using Feedback to Improve Future Proposals

Feedback is your best friend in the world of grant writing. Whether from the funder, a peer, or a mentor, constructive criticism offers invaluable insights that can dramatically improve your future proposals. To fully benefit from feedback, you must embrace it, even when it's difficult to accept.

Take the story of Rachel, a small business owner in the performing arts sector. Rachel applied for a grant to expand her dance studio but didn't make the cut. However, instead of being discouraged, she contacted the funder for feedback. They pointed out that while her project was innovative, her community impact section was underdeveloped. With this feedback, Rachel revised her approach, highlighting her studio's role in offering affordable dance classes to underprivileged communities. The result? She secured the grant in her next application.

Using feedback effectively requires you to approach it with a growth mindset. It's not about what you did wrong but how you can improve. Organizations that actively seek and incorporate feedback into their grant-writing process increase their success rates. Effectively using feedback can determine whether small businesses and individual grant seekers get funded or are left behind.

Action Items

- Integrate sustainability goals into your project objectives for long-term success.

- Reduce financial risk after the grant by diversifying your funding sources.

- Explore additional grant opportunities and other financial support options.

- Build lasting relationships with funders by engaging them regularly.

- Express genuine gratitude to funders after completing each milestone.

- Involve funders in strategic planning to deepen their investment in your project.

- Review each grant cycle thoroughly to pinpoint strengths and areas needing improvement.

- Use feedback constructively to refine and improve future grant proposals.

Continuous improvement in grant writing is about more than just trying harder next time; it's about being strategic and thoughtful in your approach. By reflecting on each grant cycle and using feedback to refine your proposals, you increase your chances of securing funding and building a stronger foundation for your project or organization's long-term success. Whether in the performing arts or running a small business, every experience is a stepping stone toward mastering the art of grant writing. Keep learning, keep improving, and the grants will follow.

Conclusion

Congratulations! You've navigated the highs and lows of the grant writing journey. Whether you're a novice or a seasoned grant writer, focus on persistence and growth rather than just obtaining funds. Each proposal you write, all the feedback you receive, and every challenge you tackle add to your knowledge and expertise. You've already demonstrated the dedication and skill needed to pursue your goals—now it's time to maintain that momentum.

Picture this scenario: You've dedicated yourself to perfecting your proposal, polishing it until it gleams. As the deadline approaches, you confidently hit "submit." The feeling of accomplishment comes from the result and the journey itself. Whether you win the grant or need to make revisions, you've moved closer to your goals. The most successful grant writers embrace the learning process and view each application as a chance to sharpen their skills and grow.

Keep trusting your vision, mission, and ability to bring it to life. You have the means, wisdom, and power to make a difference. When doubt starts to surface, remember the hard work you've invested, the progress you've achieved, and the potential ahead. You're more than a grant writer—you're a changemaker, and the world needs more individuals like you who want to follow their dreams.

Staying in Touch: Joining the Grant Writing Community

Connecting with others on the same journey is one of the best ways to stay motivated and grow as a grant writer. The grant writing community is large, with many people and associations sharing your dedication to making a difference. By joining this community, you gain valuable insights, tips, and a supportive network to help you navigate the challenges of grant writing.

Begin by joining online gatherings and forums where grant writers connect. Platforms like GrantSpace (URL: learning.candid.org) and

LinkedIn Groups (URL: linkedin.com/groups/) provide dedicated spaces for asking questions, sharing experiences, and exchanging advice. You can stay updated on the latest grant writing trends, uncover new funding opportunities, and find mentors eager to help with challenging applications. These communities are also perfect for celebrating your victories—big or small—and for finding support when you need it.

Another benefit of joining an online community is participating in discussions and webinars hosted by industry experts. These events often cover many topics, from proposal writing basics to advanced strategies for securing large grants. Use these resources to stay current on best practices and continually enhance your skills.

The grant writing community offers more than just professional development; it's also a place to build valuable relationships. Networking with fellow grant writers can lead to associations, collaborations, and new prospects. Whether you want to co-author a proposal, share resources, or exchange stories about your grant writing journey, being part of a community can significantly impact your continued success.

Pay attention to the influence of social media. Active grant-writing communities thrive on X (formerly Twitter; URL: x.com), Facebook (URL: facebook.com), and Instagram (URL: instagram.com), where you can connect with peers, follow industry leaders, and stay informed about upcoming grants and workshops. By using hashtags like #GrantWriting and #NonProfitFunding, you can discover relevant content and participate in the conversation. By engaging on these platforms, you can build your online presence and establish yourself as a knowledgeable and passionate grant writer.

Join local grant writing groups or attend industry conferences to connect with others in the field. These in-person gatherings provide a more personal way to communicate with others, share ideas, and establish lasting relationships. Whether you're attending a workshop at a local nonprofit center or a national conference like the Grant Professionals Association (GPA) Annual Conference, these events are fantastic opportunities to learn, network, and grow.

Additional Resources to Keep You Growing

Continuously learning is crucial for a grant writer's success. Numerous resources can help deepen your knowledge, refine your skills, and maintain motivation. Here are some of the best blogs and workshops to keep you moving toward your goals.

Blogs

Blogs are an excellent resource for ongoing insights and updates. Here are a few that consistently provide high-quality content for grant writers:

- **GrantWatch Blog:** GrantWatch offers a wealth of information on current funding opportunities, tips for writing proposals, and insights into the world of grants. Their blog is updated regularly and is a go-to source for staying informed about new developments in grant writing.

- **Funds for Writers by C. Hope Clark:** This blog provides practical advice from C. Hope Clark, tailored for freelance writers and small organizations, focusing on writing, finding funding, and maximizing the effectiveness of your grant applications.

- **The Nonprofit Quarterly (NPQ):** NPQ provides numerous articles on nonprofit management, fundraising, and grant-seeking strategies, making it a valuable resource for understanding the broader context of grant writing.

Workshops

Workshops offer hands-on experience and personalized feedback, making them invaluable for honing your skills.

- **The Grant Training Center (URL: granttrainingcenter.com):** Offers in-depth workshops on various aspects of grant writing, including federal grant applications, foundation proposals, and budgeting. You can access their workshops in person and online, regardless of location.

- **Grant Writing USA (URL: grantwritingusa.com):** Known for its practical, results-oriented approach, Grant Writing USA offers workshops nationwide covering everything from the basics to advanced techniques. Their focus is on helping participants write grant proposals that win funding.

- **TechSoup's Grant Writing Courses (URL: techsoup.course.tc/catalog/grant-writing-and-management/):** TechSoup provides affordable online courses for small organizations and individuals seeking to improve their grant writing skills. Their courses cover various topics, from crafting narratives to understanding funder expectations.

Final Thoughts

Grant writing constantly evolves, and there's always more to learn. Stay connected to the grant writing community, continue your education through books, blogs, and workshops, and maintain a positive, growth-oriented mindset. Doing so will enhance your chances of securing funding and developing a rewarding and impactful career.

Every proposal brings you closer to turning your vision into reality. You have the aptitudes, dedication, and resources to succeed, so implement them. Keep writing, keep learning, and keep pushing on. The grant writing world is rich with opportunities; with the right approach, they can be yours.

You've got this!

Thank You!

Thank you for reading *Grant Writing Mastery: A Complete Guide to Getting Funding and Writing Winning Proposals for Nonprofits, Community Programs, and Creative Projects.* Your time spent with these pages means so much to me. I hope the insights and examples have resonated with you and provided valuable guidance and inspiration.

If this book was helpful to you, your views and feedback are invaluable. Please take a moment to convey your insights by leaving a review. Your feedback helps me improve my work, shapes future editions of this book, and assists other readers in discovering and benefiting from it.

Thank you again for being part of this journey, and I'm excited to read your thoughts!

Appendix

A. Sample of Grant Final Report Template

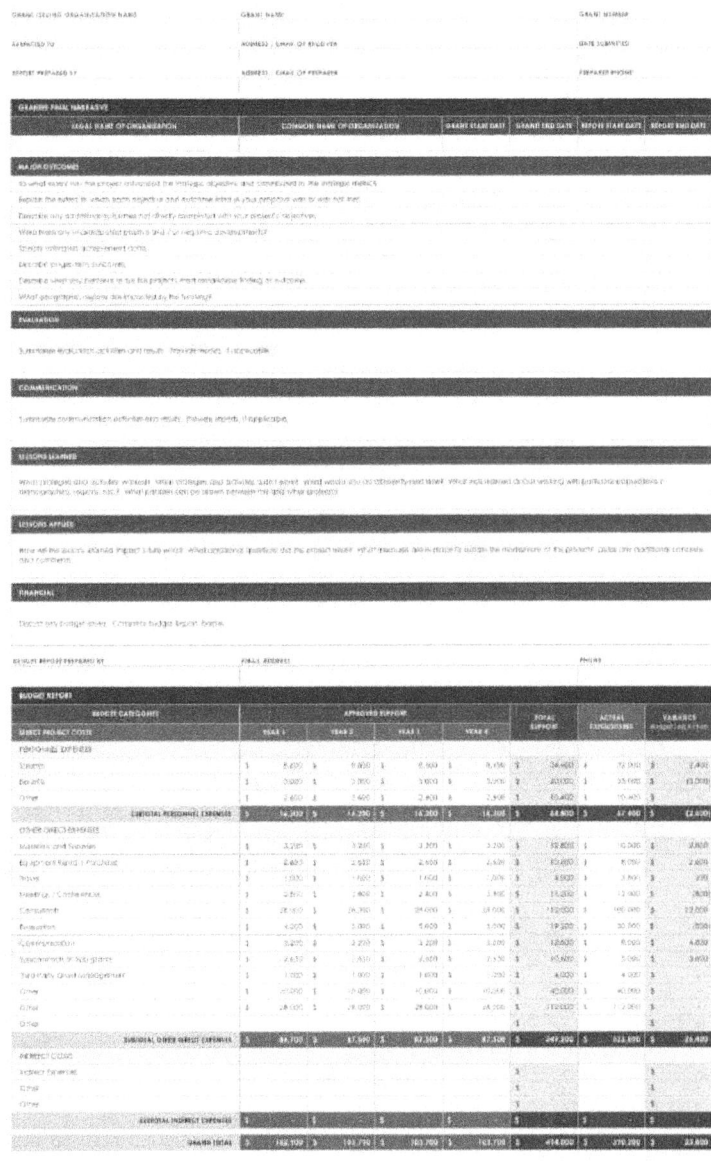

B. Project Planning Examples

Example of a SWOT Analysis

Project Title: Community Urban Gardening Initiative

- **Strengths (what we bring to the table):**
    - **Resources:**
        - We have access to unused urban lots that are perfect for gardening.
        - Our team includes enthusiastic volunteers who love gardening and community service.
        - We have partnerships with local businesses that help us with supplies and sponsorships.
    - **Skills:**
        - Our team members know their stuff regarding gardening, urban planning, and organizing community events.
        - We've successfully run educational workshops and community activities.
    - **Processes:**
        - We've established solid routines for keeping the garden healthy and rotating crops.
        - We communicate effectively with our community through social media and local newsletters.

- **Weaknesses (where we could improve):**
  - **Resources:**
    - Our budget is tight, especially for more significant projects.
    - Depending heavily on volunteers can be challenging when they are unavailable.
  - **Skills:**
    - We could use more training in advanced gardening techniques and sustainability.
    - Our marketing skills need a boost to reach a wider audience.
  - **Processes:**
    - We're still working on formalizing our project management approach.
    - Consistently coordinating volunteers and delegating tasks can be challenging.
- **Opportunities (what's out there for us):**
  - **Trends:**
    - There's a growing interest in sustainability and local food production.
    - More people are eager to learn about healthy living and environmental care.
  - **Collaborations:**
    - We can team up with local schools, universities, and environmental groups.

- - We can stand out by offering unique workshops, like those focused on native plants and organic gardening.
  - **Funding:**
    - There are potential government grants and green initiatives we can tap into.
    - Local companies may support us to fulfill their corporate social responsibility initiatives.
- **Threats (challenges we might face):**
  - **Trends:**
    - We're up against other local community projects and urban development plans.
    - It can be challenging to maintain long-term engagement with volunteers and the community.
  - **Competition:**
    - Other projects are competing for the same volunteers and funding.
    - Vandalism or theft always poses a risk in urban areas.
  - **Economic Factors:**
    - Economic downturns could make it harder to secure funding.
    - The rising cost of gardening supplies and equipment is a concern.

SWOT Analysis Summary

- Strengths include access to urban lots, enthusiastic volunteers, expertise in horticulture, and well-established communication channels.

- Weaknesses include limited financial resources, heavy reliance on volunteers, advanced training requirements, and a need for formal project management.

- Opportunities arise from the increasing interest in sustainability, demand for educational programs, collaboration potential, and available funding opportunities.

- Threats come from competition with other neighborhood projects, varying levels of volunteer interest, potential economic downturns, and rising costs.

Example of Story Mapping

Project Title: Community Urban Gardening Initiative

- **Maria's Journey to a Healthier Lifestyle**
    - **Initial challenges:** Maria's life in the city felt like a constant struggle against isolation and poor health. Surrounded by concrete and convenience stores, she longed for the vibrant, fresh flavors of fruits and vegetables. She remained stuck in a cycle of eating processed meals. Each day, she faced the mounting toll on her body—obesity, high blood pressure, and a deepening sense of despair. The weight of loneliness pressed down on her as she yearned for connection and the knowledge to nourish herself and her family. Maria's dreams of health and community seemed as distant as the nearest fresh produce—just out of reach.

- **Intervention:** Maria's life took a turn when she discovered urban gardening through the Community Urban Gardening Initiative. Joining the program was a pivotal moment. She received training in sustainable gardening practices, and volunteers helped her set up a small garden plot near her apartment. The initiative provided her with seeds, tools, and ongoing support through workshops and community meetings, playing a crucial role in her transformation.

- **Positive Outcomes:** Maria's transformation was not just personal but also communal. By incorporating fresh vegetables from her garden into her diet, she dramatically improved her health, losing weight, lowering her blood pressure, and gaining more energy. Her emotional well-being enhanced as she found belonging among fellow gardeners and actively participated in local events. Her gardening skills and healthier lifestyle boosted her self-confidence and inspired her neighbors to join the initiative. This ripple effect from her transformation sparked a wave of positive change and community spirit, demonstrating how the Community Urban Gardening Initiative can transform individual lives and entire communities.

Example of a Detailed Project Description

Project Title: Youth Soccer Skills Development Program

The Youth Soccer Skills Development Program enhances middle school students' athletic abilities and personal growth through structured soccer training, fitness routines, and team-building activities. The program aims to create a supportive and engaging environment that promotes physical fitness, skill development, and the values of teamwork and sportsmanship.

Project Overview

- **Why:** This project is crucial for providing youth with opportunities for physical activity, personal growth, and community engagement, helping to foster a healthy, active lifestyle. It directly addresses the rising levels of inactivity among young people by engaging them in a structured and supportive environment where they can develop athletic and life skills.

- **Why now:** With growing concerns about childhood obesity and the impact of sedentary lifestyles, the timing is perfect for implementing this program. The current school year offers an ideal opportunity to establish regular physical activity habits, and the upcoming sports season provides a motivating context for youth participation and success.

- **Who:** The program will involve 100 middle school students (ages 11–14) from the local community, supported by a team of experienced coaches, fitness trainers, and administrative staff. These students will be selected based on their interest in soccer and commitment to personal development. The coaching team, consisting of professionals with a background in youth sports, will ensure a positive and impactful experience for all participants.

- **How:** The initiative will involve regular training sessions, fitness activities, and competitive matches. The training will help players develop their soccer skills, improve physical fitness, and build teamwork and discipline. Fitness activities will cover conditioning exercises, strength training, and agility drills. Participants will then apply their skills in competitive matches that simulate real-world scenarios. The program will also include personal development workshops on goal-setting, leadership, and healthy living.

- **What:** This comprehensive development initiative is designed to improve soccer skills, physical fitness, and personal development through regular training sessions, fitness activities, and competitive matches. The program seeks to instill a love for the sport while fostering community and participant teamwork. It provides a structured environment where youth can thrive both on and off the field, with a focus on holistic development.

- **When:** The program runs for 12 months, from September to August, with sessions every two weeks. Training sessions are scheduled around the school calendar to help participants balance their academic responsibilities and program commitments. We plan yearly tournaments and workshops to encourage engagement and enthusiasm.

- **Where:** Activities will occur at the community soccer fields for outdoor sessions and at the local community center for indoor sessions. The community soccer fields offer ample space for training and matches. In contrast, the community center provides a controlled environment for fitness activities and workshops. Participants can easily access both locations, ensuring transportation does not hinder their participation.

Objectives and Goals

The program aims to improve participants' soccer skills by 30% through structured training sessions. It seeks to boost overall physical fitness levels using customized fitness routines. Additionally, the program focuses on instilling values of teamwork and sportsmanship through collaborative activities and competitive matches.

Beneficiaries

The program's primary beneficiaries are 100 middle school students who will directly participate. The local community also benefits from increased youth engagement and reduced juvenile delinquency.

Specific Outcomes

Participants will improve their soccer skills, measured through standardized skill assessments. Their physical fitness levels will be enhanced and documented using fitness tests. The program will also foster the development of teamwork and sportsmanship qualities among all participants.

Activities

The program will conduct biweekly soccer training sessions to improve dribbling, passing, shooting, and defensive skills. Regular fitness activities, including endurance runs, strength training, and agility drills, will be part of the routine. Monthly competitive matches with local teams will provide opportunities to apply and test the skills learned. Additionally, educational workshops will cover nutrition, injury prevention, and mental health topics.

Timeline

- **Phase 1:** Planning and preparation (month 1-2)
    - **Weeks 1–2:** Conduct outreach and complete initial surveys.
    - **Week 3:** Finalize the project team and secure venues and suppliers.
    - **Week 4:** Develop a detailed project plan, schedule, and budget; hold initial parent meetings.
- **Phase 2:** Program launch (month 3)
    - **Week 1:** Host the kick-off event; distribute uniforms and materials.
    - **Weeks 2-4:** Begin regular training sessions; monitor attendance and gather feedback.
- **Phase 3:** Program implementation (months 4–9)

- - Hold biweekly training sessions and monthly progress meetings.
  - Conduct a mid-program evaluation and feedback session.

- **Phase 4:** Evaluation and adjustment (month 10)

  - Collect data and analyze the results; review findings and make necessary adjustments.

- **Phase 5:** Final phase and program conclusion (months 11–12)

  - Conduct final training sessions and skill assessments.
  - Host a closing event with friendly matches and an award ceremony; compile the final report.

Resources Required

- **Personnel:** Ensure the program's success by recruiting individuals with relevant experience and expertise. Roles and qualifications will be clearly defined to attract top candidates for positions like Program Director, Head Coach, Assistant Coach, Fitness Trainer, and Program Coordinator.

- **Materials:** Provide necessary items, including soccer balls, cones, bibs, goals, fitness equipment, first aid kits, and uniforms.

- **Facilities:** Utilize community soccer fields for outdoor activities and the community center for indoor sessions.

- **Funding:** Secure funds to cover the costs of salaries, equipment, travel, facility rentals, and administrative expenses.

Methodologies

- **Training sessions:** Conduct structured drills and exercises to develop fundamental and advanced soccer skills.

- **Fitness routines:** Incorporate endurance, strength, and agility training to boost physical fitness and encourage positive mental development.

- **Assessments:** Administer standardized skill and fitness tests and regular one-on-one check-ins with players to track progress.

- **Feedback mechanisms:** Collect feedback consistently from coaches, parents, and participants to improve the program.

Example of a Poorly Written Budget

Category	Amount
Salaries	$10,000
Materials	$5,000
Travel	$2,000
Indirect costs	$3,000
Total	$20,000

Issues With This Budget

- **Lack of detail:** The broad budget categories create confusion about the specific items or services included.

- **No justification:** There is no explanation or rationale for the amounts listed.

- **Inaccurate estimations:** It's hard to verify if the amounts are reasonable or accurate without detailed breakdowns.

- **Alignment with project scope:** The budget does not connect the expenses to the project's specific activities and objectives.

Example of a Well-Written Budget

Project Title: Youth Soccer Skills Development Program

Category	Description	Amount
Salaries		
Program Director	20 hours/week @ $25/hour for 12 months	$26,000
Head Coach	15 hours/week @ $20/hour for 12 months	$15,600
Assistant Coach	10 hours/week @ $15/hour for 12 months	$7,800
Fitness Trainer	5 hours/week @ $30/hour for 12 months	$7,800
Program Coordinator	10 hours/week @ $18/hour for 12 months	$9,360
Materials		
Soccer Equipment	Balls, cones, bibs, goals	$2,500
Training Supplies	Fitness equipment, first aid kits	$1,000
Uniforms	Uniforms for participants	$2,000

Travel			
	Local Travel	Mileage for staff attending local schools and events (500 miles @ $0.58/mile)	$290
Indirect Costs			
	Facility Rental	Weekly rental for training sessions	$3,600
	Administrative Costs	Office supplies, utilities	$1,200
Total			$77,150

Strengths of This Budget

- **Detailed breakdown:** Breaks down each category into specific items and quantities to clarify the included items.

- **Justification:** Each expense is justified by explaining the cost and the need within the project.

- **Accurate estimations:** The detailed approach allows for precise cost estimations and better planning.

- **Alignment with project scope:** The budget aligns with the project's objectives and activities, showing how each cost contributes to the overall goal.

Funders gain confidence in the practical and transparent use of their investment when they see a well-written budget that demonstrates thorough planning.

Example of a Pie Chart

Project Title: Youth Soccer Skills Development Program

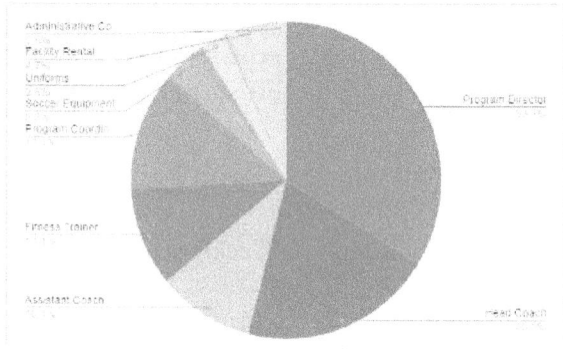

Category	Amount
Salaries	
Program Director	$26,000
Head Coach	$15,600
Assistant Coach	$7,800
Fitness Trainer	$7,800
Program Coordinator	$9,360
Materials	
Soccer Equipment	$2,500
Training Supplies	$1,000
Uniforms	$2,000
Travel	
Local Travel	$290
Indirect Costs	
Facility Rental	$3,600
Administrative Costs	$1,200
Total	$77,150

Example of a Timeline

Project Title: Youth Soccer Skills Development Program

Phase 1: Planning and Preparation (Month 1–2)

Month 1:

- **Week 1–2:** Conduct community outreach and initial surveys to identify participants and gauge interest.

- **Week 3:** Finalize the project team and assign roles. Secure venue and equipment suppliers.

- **Week 4:** Develop a detailed project plan, schedule, and budget. Conduct initial parent meetings.

Month 2:

- **Week 1:** Obtain necessary permits and insurance.

- **Week 2:** Order equipment and materials. Finalize curriculum and training modules.

- **Week 3–4:** Hold staff training sessions and mock drills. Finalize participant registrations and schedules.

Phase 2: Program Launch (Month 3)

Month 3:

- **Week 1:** Kick-off event with parents and participants. Distribute uniforms and materials.
- **Week 2–4:** Begin regular training sessions twice a week. Monitor attendance and initial feedback.

Phase 3: Program Implementation (Months 4-9)

Month 4–5:

- Conduct biweekly training sessions focusing on fundamental skills and physical fitness.
- Hold weekly progress meetings with staff to address any issues.

Month 6–7:

- Introduce advanced skills and tactical training—mid-program evaluation and feedback session with participants and parents.

Month 8–9:

- Continue training sessions. Organize friendly matches with local teams to assess skill development.

Phase 4: Evaluation and Adjustment (Month 10)

Month 10:

- **Week 1–2:** Collect and analyze data on participants' progress. Conduct interviews and surveys with participants and parents.

- **Week 3:** Review findings with the coaching staff and make necessary adjustments to the program.
- **Week 4:** Implement any changes and prepare for the final phase.

Phase 5: Final Phase and Program Conclusion (Month 11-12)

Month 11:

- Continue training sessions with a focus on consolidating skills.
- Prepare participants for the final assessment.

Month 12:

- **Week 1:** Conduct final skill assessment and evaluation.
- **Week 2:** Organize a closing event with friendly matches and an award ceremony.
- **Week 3–4:** Compile final report and feedback for future improvements. Submit a report to funders.

By outlining a detailed timeline, you demonstrate the structured approach and careful planning necessary to ensure the successful completion of your project within the grant period. This not only shows the feasibility of your project but also helps build the grant reviewer's confidence in your ability to execute it successfully.

Example of an Evaluation Plan

Project Title: Youth Soccer Skills Development Program

Evaluation Plan

- **Objectives:**

- o Improve the soccer skills of participants by 30% within 12 months.
- o Increase participants' physical fitness levels.
- o Promote teamwork and sportsmanship among participants.

- **Metrics and Methods:**
  - o **Skill Improvement:**
    - **Metric:** Standardized skill tests to measure soccer skill levels.
    - **Method:** Conduct skill assessments before, during, and after the program, covering dribbling, passing, shooting, and defensive maneuvers. Administer tests at the beginning, midpoint, and conclusion of the program.
    - **Tool:** Standardized soccer skill assessment checklist.
  - o **Physical Fitness:**
    - **Metric:** Demonstration of participants' physical fitness levels through endurance, strength, and agility.
    - **Method:** At the beginning, middle, and end of the program, utilize fitness tests such as the Cooper Test (12-minute run), push-up test, and agility drills.
    - **Tool:** Fitness tracking forms and physical fitness test scores.
  - o **Teamwork and Sportsmanship:**

- **Metric:** Qualitative feedback of teamwork and sportsmanship.
- **Method:** Gather insights on developing teamwork and sportsmanship by conducting surveys and interviews with participants, parents, and coaches.
- **Tool:** Custom survey forms and interview guides.

- **Data Collection and Analysis:**
    - **Frequency:** We will collect data at three key points: the start of the program (baseline), six months (mid-term), and 12 months (end-term).
    - **Data analysis:** Quantitative data (skill tests and fitness scores) will be analyzed using statistical methods to determine percentage improvements. Qualitative data (survey and interview responses) will be coded and analyzed for common themes and insights.

- **Reporting:**
    - **Progress reports:** We will prepare monthly progress reports to monitor ongoing activities and make necessary adjustments.
    - **Final report:** A comprehensive final report will summarize the findings, achievements, and lessons learned. This report will include detailed analysis, graphs, and testimonials from participants and parents.

- **Feedback Loop:**
    - **Adjustments:** Based on evaluation findings, we will adjust the program to address any identified weaknesses and enhance the effectiveness of the interventions.

- **Continuous improvement:** To ensure continuous improvement of the program, regular feedback sessions will be held with coaches and participants.

Summary: This evaluation plan systematically assesses the effectiveness of the Youth Soccer Skills Development Program. It uses quantitative and qualitative methods to thoroughly examine the program's impact on participants' soccer skills, physical fitness, and personal development. The plan includes structured data collection, analysis, and regular reporting, clearly showing a commitment to consistently evaluating and improving the project.

C. Grant Application Checklist Template

This straightforward grant application checklist template includes all the essential components. You can tailor it to fit the particular grant requirements you're adhering to.

Grant Application Checklist

- **Eligibility Criteria**

[ ] Confirm the organization's or individual's eligibility.

[ ] Ensure your proposal matches the funder's goals and key objectives.

[ ] Verify geographic, demographic, or other specific eligibility requirements.

- **Required Documents**

[ ] Completed application form.

[ ] Executive summary or project overview.

[ ] Detailed project description or narrative.

[ ] Budget and financial information.

[ ] Letters of support or references.

[ ] Proof of nonprofit status or other relevant legal documentation.

[ ] Resumes or CVs of key personnel.

[ ] The funder may request more documents.

- **Formatting Specifications**

[ ] Follow specific formatting guidelines (font type, size, margins, etc.).

[ ] Include required headers and footers on each page.

[ ] Ensure proper pagination.

[ ] Check for any word or page limits.

- **Submission Deadlines**

[ ] Identify the final submission deadline.

[ ] Confirm time zone considerations if submitting online.

[ ] Set internal deadlines for draft reviews and approvals.

[ ] Plan for delivery (mail, courier, or online submission).

[ ] Ensure all attachments are correctly labeled and included in the correct format (PDF, word doc, etc.).

- **Review and Finalize**

[ ] Proofread for grammar, spelling, and clarity.

[ ] Make sure you complete all sections of the application.

[ ] Obtain necessary signatures or approvals.

[ ] Save a copy of the final submission for your records.

- **Submission Confirmation**

[ ] Receive and save confirmation of submission (email or receipt).

[ ] Follow up with the funder if no confirmation is received.

Use this checklist to ensure you complete and submit all critical components of your grant application correctly, boosting your chances of success.

D. Example of an Evaluation Plan

Project Title: Empowering a Local Minority Woman-Owned Bakery: Business Expansion and Community Engagement

Objective: To evaluate the impact of the grant on the business growth, community engagement, and overall success of a minority woman-owned bakery.

Process Evaluation

Objective: Assess the implementation and effectiveness of the business expansion strategies supported by the grant.

Key Questions:

- How effectively were the grant funds utilized in the business expansion?
    - **What it's measuring:** The appropriateness and timeliness of fund allocation for intended purposes like equipment purchase, marketing, and hiring.
    - **Success looks like:** Funds allocated according to the budget plan, resulting in successful procurement and implementation of necessary business resources.
    - **Qualitative methods:** Interviews with the business owner to discuss the process of fund allocation and any challenges encountered.

- ○ **Quantitative methods:** Reviews of financial records and budgets to analyze spending against the planned allocation.

- Was the marketing strategy implemented successfully to attract new customers?

    - ○ **What it's measuring:** The effectiveness of marketing efforts funded by the grant.

    - ○ **Success looks like:** Increased customer footfall, social media engagement, and online sales.

    - ○ **Qualitative methods:** Customer feedback gathered through interviews or focus groups about how they discovered the bakery.

    - ○ **Quantitative methods:** Analysis of social media analytics, customer footfall data, and sales figures before and after the marketing campaign.

- Did the bakery effectively connect with the local community through events or collaborations?

    - ○ **What it's measuring:** The level of community engagement and partnership building.

    - ○ **Success looks like:** Participation in at least two community events and forming at least one local partnership.

    - ○ **Qualitative methods:** Interviews with the business owner and community members about the events and partnerships.

    - ○ **Quantitative methods:** Records of the number of events hosted/attended and partnerships formed.

Results Evaluation

Objective: Evaluate the results and lasting effects of the grant on the business.

Key Questions:

- Did the grant help boost company earnings and profitability?
    - **What it's measuring:** The financial growth of the business post-grant.
    - **Success looks like:** A measurable increase in monthly revenue and profitability within six months of receiving the grant.
    - **Qualitative methods:** Case studies that include interviews with the business owner about the financial changes and strategies implemented.
    - **Quantitative methods:** Comparisons of pre- and post-grant financial statements to measure increases in revenue and profit margins.
- How did the grant impact the bakery's ability to serve a broader customer base, including underserved communities?
    - **What it's measuring:** The expansion of the customer base and inclusivity in service.
    - **Success looks like:** An increase in the number of customers from underserved communities and improved customer satisfaction.
    - **Qualitative methods:** Feedback gathered from customers in underserved communities to gain insights into their experiences.
    - **Quantitative methods:** Records of customer demographics and satisfaction surveys before and after the expansion.
- Did the business experience growth in brand recognition and customer loyalty?

- **What it's measuring:** The development of brand visibility and customer loyalty.

- **Success looks like:** Increased brand recognition in the community, reflected in repeat customers and social media following.

- **Qualitative methods:** Interviews with repeat customers to understand their loyalty to the brand and reasons for continued patronage.

- **Quantitative methods:** Analysis of changes in social media followers, repeat purchase rates, and customer retention data.

• Were new job opportunities created as a result of the business expansion?

- **What it's measuring:** The grant's impact on business employment.

- **Success looks like:** The creation of at least one new full-time or part-time job within six months of receiving the grant.

- **Qualitative methods:** Interviews with new employees about their experiences and the opportunities provided by the business.

- **Quantitative methods:** Records of the number of jobs created and compare employee headcount before and after the grant.

Long-Term Impact Evaluation

Objective: Assess the sustained impact of the grant on business sustainability and community influence.

Key Questions:

- How has the business maintained or improved its performance one year after receiving the grant?
    - **What it's measuring:** The sustainability of the business's growth and operations.
    - **Success looks like:** Continued growth in revenue, customer base, and community engagement one year post-grant.
    - **Qualitative methods:** Follow-up interviews conducted with the business owner and key community stakeholders to discuss long-term changes.
    - **Quantitative methods:** Analysis of long-term financial performance data and customer engagement metrics.
- Did the bakery contribute to economic development in the local community?
    - **What it's measuring:** The business's role in supporting local economic growth.
    - **Success looks like:** Increased local economic activity, evidenced by new local partnerships or collaborations.
    - **Qualitative methods:** Interviews with community leaders and local business owners about the bakery's impact on the community.
    - **Quantitative methods:** Records of new business activities, collaborations, and economic indicators in the community over time.

This evaluation plan provides a comprehensive framework for measuring the effectiveness and impact of the grant on the minority woman-owned bakery, ensuring both the business and the grant's objectives are met and sustained.

E. Letter of Support Sample

Example Letter of Support:

February 1, 2006

Ms. Mary E. Wilfert
NCAA CHOICES Program
P.O. Box 6222
Indianapolis, Indiana 46206-6222

Dear Ms. Wilfert:

It is my pleasure write a letter in support of the proposal (name) being submitted to the CHOICES Program by our (name dept) at Albion College.

Something here about writer's relationship/knowledge of situation and how project/program will impact it.

In conclusion, I fully support the efforts of the (Dept) as they seek external funding to support a program designed to (whatever you are targeting). EX "Any programs that can help our students make better decisions about drinking and its consequences will benefit our students, campus, and the community at large." In other words, you need a very concise and strong closing summary statement.

Sincerely,

(original signature "John Doe" here)

John Doe
Vice President for Student Affairs

References

About grant writer success rates. (2018, August 16). Funding for Good. https://fundingforgood.org/about-grant-writer-success-rates/

American Express supports small and independent restaurants around the world with two "Backing Small" grant programs. (2023, June 2). Resy. https://blog.resy.com/newsroom/backing-historic-small-restaurants-2023/

Berg, J. M., Wrzesniewski, A., Grant, A. M., Kurkoski, J., & Welle, B. (2022, May 12). Getting unstuck: The effects of growth mindsets about the self and job on happiness at work. *Journal of Applied Psychology* 108(1), 152–166. https://pubmed.ncbi.nlm.nih.gov/35549284/

Chan, E. S. M., Shero, J. A., Hand, E. D., Cole, A. M., Gaye, F., Spiegel, J. A., & Kofler, M. J (2023, February 23). Are reading interventions effective for at-risk readers with ADHD? A meta-analysis. *Journal of Attention Disorder* 27(2), 182–200. https://journals.sagepub.com/doi/10.1177/10870547221130111

11 things about grant writing you may not have known. (2021, July 15). Wave Accounting. https://www.waveapps.com/freelancing/grant-writing-things-to-know

Free grants and programs for small business. (2024, July 26). U.S. Chamber of Commerce. https://www.uschamber.com/co/run/business-financing/small-business-grants-and-programs

Fuller, J. (2020, May 6). *Google $100 million coronavirus grant to provide relief.* The Keyword. https://blog.google/outreach-initiatives/google-org/100-million-dollar-contribution-covid-19-relief/

Grants & funding. (n.d.). National Institutes of Health (NIH). https://www.nih.gov/grants-funding

Grant writing facts every board member should know. (2020, March 3). Funding for Good. https://fundingforgood.org/grant-writing-facts-every-board-member-should-know/

How infographics can help your business. (2017, December 15). Digital Information World. https://www.digitalinformationworld.com/2017/12/how-infographics-can-help-your-business.html

How your board contributes to the grant winning process. (2019, September 24). Funding for Good. https://fundingforgood.org/how-your-board-contributes-to-the-grant-winning-process/

Kotloff, L. J., & Burd, N. (2012, April). *Building stronger nonprofits through better financial management: Early efforts in 26 youth-serving organizations.* Wallace Foundation. https://wallacefoundation.org/sites/default/files/2023-08/Building-Stronger-Nonprofits-Through-Better-Financial-Management.pdf

Lindeman, D. H. (2020, April 30). *Going for the grant: Strategies and tips for editing grant proposals.* ACES: The Society for Editing. https://aceseditors.org/news/2020/going-for-the-grant-strategies-and-tips-for-editing-grant-proposals

Marker, A. (2018, February 1). *Free grant proposal templates.* Smartsheet. https://www.smartsheet.com/free-grant-proposal-templates

Mental health by the numbers. (2023, April). National Alliance of Mental Illness. https://www.nami.org/About-Mental-Illness/Mental-Health-By-the-Numbers/

National Endowment for the Arts supports the arts with over $27.5 million in awards in first round of FY2021 funding. (2021, February 4).

National Endowment for the Arts. https://www.arts.gov/news/press-releases/2021/national-endowment-arts-supports-arts-over-275-million-awards-first-round-fy2021-funding

Nielsen, J. (2010, October 31). *Photos as web content.* Nielsen Norman Group. https://www.nngroup.com/articles/photos-as-web-content/

Our grants program. (n.d.). Clif Family Foundation. https://cliffamilyfoundation.org/grants-program

Pavic, H. (2023, May 22). *The role of storytelling in grant writing.* Lakewood University. https://lakewood.edu/2023/05/the-role-of-storytelling-in-grant-writing/

Rock, J. (2021, July 26). *Schumer announces New York's latest semiconductor deal, to subsidy watchdogs' chagrin.* New York Focus. https://nysfocus.com/2021/07/26/schumer-globalfoundries-semiconductor-subsidies/

The Rockefeller Foundation commits over usd 1 billion to advance climate solutions. (2023, September 15). The Rockefeller Foundation. https://www.rockefellerfoundation.org/news/the-rockefeller-foundation-commits-over-usd-1-billion-to-advance-climate-solutions/

Santoro, H. (2021, November 1). *The daunting but vital world of grant writing.* American Psychological Association. https://www.apa.org/monitor/2021/11/career-grant-writing

Statement from Gates Foundation CEO Mark Suzman: No barriers should stand in the way of equitable vaccine access. (n.d.). Bill & Melinda Gates Foundation. https://www.gatesfoundation.org/ideas/media-center/press-releases/2021/05/covid-vaccine-access

What types of federal grants are made to state and local governments and how do they work? (n.d.). Tax Policy Center. https://www.taxpolicycenter.org/briefing-book/what-types-federal-grants-are-made-state-and-local-governments-and-how-do-they-work

Wilcox, K. (2023, February 17). *The impact of ADHD on academic performance.* Psychology Today. https://www.psychologytoday.com/us/blog/mythbusting-adhd/202302/the-impact-of-adhd-on-academic-performance

About the Author

Hoong Yee Lee is a grant writing expert with over 15 years of experience, both as a funder and a grants reviewer, having awarded more than $10 million in funding. With deep insider knowledge of what appeals to grant reviewers, Hoong Yee offers a unique perspective that helps readers craft proposals that stand out. She has helped nonprofits, community programs, and artists secure essential funding to bring their visions to life. Her clear, practical strategies are designed to guide readers through the entire grant writing process, empowering them to create winning proposals that get results.

www.ingramcontent.com/pod-product-compliance
Lightning Source LLC
Chambersburg PA
CBHW060507030426
42337CB00015B/1775